POCAHONTAS

A Life in Two Worlds

Victoria Garrett Jones

STERLING

New York / London
www.sterlingpublishing.com/kids

I would like to dedicate this book to the memory of my cousin Edward Spencer Garrett Jr. with love and appreciation for his wonderful sense of humor and great generosity of spirit.

STERLING and the distinctive Sterling logo are registered trademarks of Sterling Publishing Co., Inc.

Library of Congress Cataloging-in-Publication Data
Jones, Victoria Garrett.
  Pocahontas : a life in two worlds / by Victoria Garrett Jones.
     p. cm. — (Sterling biographies)
  Includes bibliographical references and index.
  ISBN 978-1-4027-5158-5 (pbk.) — ISBN 978-1-4027-6844-6 (hardcover)
  1. Pocahontas, d. 1617—Juvenile literature. 2. Powhatan Indians—Biography—Juvenile literature. 3. Jamestown (Va.)—History—Juvenile literature. I. Title.
  E99.P85P57422 2010
  975.5'01092—dc22
  [B]
                                                                    2009024136

Lot#: 10 9 8 7 6 5 4 3 2 1
03/10

Published by Sterling Publishing Co., Inc.
387 Park Avenue South, New York, NY 10016
© 2010 by Victoria Garrett Jones

Distributed in Canada by Sterling Publishing
c/o Canadian Manda Group, 165 Dufferin Street
Toronto, Ontario, Canada M6K 3H6
Distributed in the United Kingdom by GMC Distribution Services
Castle Place, 166 High Street, Lewes, East Sussex, England BN7 1XU
Distributed in Australia by Capricorn Link (Australia) Pty. Ltd.
P.O. Box 704, Windsor, NSW 2756, Australia

Printed in China

Sterling ISBN 978-1-4027-5158-5 (paperback)
        ISBN 978-1-4027-6844-6 (hardcover)

Image research by Larry Schwartz

For information about custom editions, special sales, premium and corporate purchases, please contact Sterling Special Sales Department at 800-805-5489 or specialsales@sterlingpublishing.com.

Contents

Events in the Life of Pocahontas

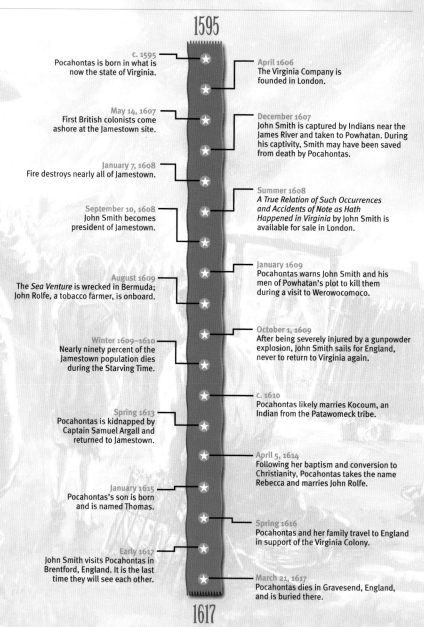

1595

c. 1595
Pocahontas is born in what is now the state of Virginia.

April 1606
The Virginia Company is founded in London.

May 14, 1607
First British colonists come ashore at the Jamestown site.

December 1607
John Smith is captured by Indians near the James River and taken to Powhatan. During his captivity, Smith may have been saved from death by Pocahontas.

January 7, 1608
Fire destroys nearly all of Jamestown.

Summer 1608
A True Relation of Such Occurrences and Accidents of Note as Hath Happened in Virginia by John Smith is available for sale in London.

September 10, 1608
John Smith becomes president of Jamestown.

January 1609
Pocahontas warns John Smith and his men of Powhatan's plot to kill them during a visit to Werowocomoco.

August 1609
The *Sea Venture* is wrecked in Bermuda; John Rolfe, a tobacco farmer, is onboard.

October 1, 1609
After being severely injured by a gunpowder explosion, John Smith sails for England, never to return to Virginia again.

Winter 1609–1610
Nearly ninety percent of the Jamestown population dies during the Starving Time.

c. 1610
Pocahontas likely marries Kocoum, an Indian from the Patawomeck tribe.

Spring 1613
Pocahontas is kidnapped by Captain Samuel Argall and returned to Jamestown.

April 5, 1614
Following her baptism and conversion to Christianity, Pocahontas takes the name Rebecca and marries John Rolfe.

January 1615
Pocahontas's son is born and is named Thomas.

Spring 1616
Pocahontas and her family travel to England in support of the Virginia Colony.

Early 1617
John Smith visits Pocahontas in Brentford, England. It is the last time they will see each other.

March 21, 1617
Pocahontas dies in Gravesend, England, and is buried there.

1617

Different Worlds

During the time of two or three [years], she . . . next,
under God, was still the instrument to preserve the
[Colony] from death, famine, and utter confusion. . . .

—*John Smith writing about Pocahontas to England's*
Queen Anne, 1616

When Chief Japazaws and his wife encouraged Pocahontas to join them for a meal aboard the English ship, the *Treasurer*, she agreed. But later, resting onboard, Pocahontas felt uneasy. Perhaps it was an inborn mistrust of the European strangers who had come to settle in the land of her people. Although some—like John Smith—had seemed friendly, others had made war, destroyed villages, and stolen food. Whatever the reason, Pocahontas suddenly knew she had to get off the ship and return with her friends to the safety of shore.

But she was too late. She had been betrayed by Japazaws who had traded the young woman for the price of a shiny copper kettle. Pocahontas was now a **hostage** held for **ransom** by her English captors. As word was sent to her father, the great Chief Powhatan, the young woman's fate hung in the balance. Would Powhatan pay the ransom?

Although Pocahontas did not live very long, the story of the Powhatan princess from the woodlands of Virginia has touched many lives. While myth and legend have clouded some of the details, what remains is a life of bravery and unselfishness, and a commitment to peace that has served as an inspiration to others.

CHAPTER 1

The Powhatan People

History is the memory of time, the life of the dead, and the happiness of the living.
—*John Smith, 1630*

The "New World" into which the earliest settlers of Jamestown sailed in 1607 was, in truth, an old one. People had been living in the area for thousands of years. In the early seventeenth century, those who populated the forested woodlands of what would become known as Virginia were entirely different from the English strangers they called *tassantassas*. These forest-dwelling groups were the people of Pocahontas—a nation of Algonquian-speaking tribes who had been living along the shores of the Chesapeake Bay for three centuries.

As the seventeenth century began, settlers prepared to sail from the English shore to the lands of the Virginia Tidewater. A mighty chief named Wahunsenacah ruled over the Tidewater region—overseeing some fourteen thousand people. Today he is more commonly known as Powhatan.

Depicted in an early hand-colored engraving, these Roanoke Island natives were among the first Indians encountered by English settlers.

Named for a Queen

Despite the fact that the Powhatan and other Native American tribes had resided in the area for hundreds—perhaps thousands—of years, the English were quick to claim ownership and rename the lands they began to explore in the late sixteenth century. On March 25, 1584, Sir Walter Raleigh was granted permission by the British monarch Elizabeth I to discover "remote, heathen, and barbarous lands . . . not actually possessed of any Christian prince or inhabited by Christian people," and to take possession of them in the name of the queen. Due to her unmarried state, Elizabeth I was popularly referred to as the Virgin Queen. Raleigh is believed to have proposed *Virginia* as the name for these undiscovered territories in her honor. The name was originally used by the British in reference to all unexplored lands stretching westward from the Atlantic coastline to the Mississippi River and beyond.

Ruler of England from 1558 to 1603, Elizabeth I never married. Today's state of Virginia owes its name to this "Virgin Queen."

Powhatan's towering strength and regal manner are dramatically portrayed in this contemporary sculpture from today's Jamestown Settlement Museum in Williamsburg, Virginia.

English settler John Smith met Powhatan in 1608 and wrote that he was "a tall, well-proportioned man, with a [sour] look, his head somewhat gray, his beard so [thin], that it [seemed] none at all, his age [near sixty], of a very able and hardy body . . ." William Strachey, an early Jamestown colonist, described him as "well beaten with many cold and stormy winters" but "of a tall stature and clean limbs."

As the ruler of such a vast empire, Powhatan amassed large amounts of **tribute** from his people. "It is strange to see with what great fear and adoration all these people do obey this Powhatan, for at his feet they present whatsoever he commands," wrote Strachey. By one estimate, the chief collected approximately 80 percent of the foods and goods his people produced. Alternately described as intelligent and energetic as well as fearsome and majestic, Powhatan was able to support a large family due to his great wealth and extensive empire. He may have had more than one hundred wives and dozens of offspring. Among them was the child Pocahontas.

Her Father's Favorite

While no record exists confirming the exact date of Pocahontas's birth, most historians believe she was born in 1595. Much of her story is interwoven with myth and folklore—poems, songs, stories, paintings, plays, and movies have all celebrated her life. Despite the lack of specific historical information about much of her story, all writers agree that, among her father's many children, she clearly was the favorite.

Nothing at all is known about Pocahontas's mother. Usually, following tribal tradition, when the great chief Powhatan chose a woman to marry, her royal status was only temporary. Once she gave birth to her first child, Powhatan usually had nothing more to do with her and moved on to his next choice of spouse. While Pocahontas probably spent her very earliest years with her mother, tradition held that by no later than age three or four, she would have been taken away and brought to live in Powhatan's household.

Much of her story is interwoven with myth and folklore . . .

As was the custom among the Powhatan Indians (as well as among many other Native American groups, such as the Navajo), Pocahontas was given a special tribal name by her clan at birth.

The child Pocahontas is depicted outside her woodland home in this illustration from an early 20th-century biography.

By tradition, this name generally was kept secret outside a child's immediate family or clan, not used in everyday life, and considered part of one's own special, magical being. The name chosen for Powhatan's favorite daughter was Matoaka (or Matowaka), which is believed to mean "Little Snow Feather." The reason for this choice was known only to those of her tribe, and one can only speculate as to its significance. Perhaps the name may give a clue to the time of year in which this special child was born. But Pocahontas was the child's public name, and how she was—and still is—most commonly known. A public name usually described some characteristic of a child's personality. Historians believe that it was Powhatan himself who selected the name *Pocahontas*, which meant "frisky, playful, or mischievous" in the tribe's native language.

Sailing westward from Spain late in the fifteenth century, Christopher Columbus hoped to find a new route to the Indies (the name then given to parts of Asia). Instead, he found the North American continent blocking his path. Even though he had not reached his intended destination, Columbus still referred to the native peoples he encountered on the far side of the Atlantic as "Indians." Four centuries later, the term was still in use, but more commonly appeared as "*American* Indian" to avoid confusion with people from India. By the middle of the last century, many people felt that the term "Native American" was more accurate. In 1995, a government survey of members of this ethnic group found that about 50 percent preferred being called "American Indian" while about 38 percent chose "Native American." Both terms are in regular use today and personal preference should be a guiding factor.

Birthplace of Pocahontas

Although the Powhatan nation encompassed eight thousand square miles and was made up of many villages, it is believed that Pocahontas was most likely born at Werowocomoco, the site of her father's primary residence in the years before the settlement of Jamestown. (*Werowocomoco* meant "rich—or royal—court" in Algonquian.)

Typically, major villages included a large house where the chief and his family lived, storage buildings used mainly for holding food, various home sites, and a council building where

Seat of Powhatan power and birthplace of Pocahontas, the village of Werowocomoco (circled on map) is sited on John Smith's 1612 map of Virginia.

tribal meetings were held. All of this might be surrounded by a palisade (a log wall used for protection). Since there were no domesticated animals such as cows, sheep, goats, or horses (these would all come with the Europeans), there was little need for other fences or enclosures. The village of Werowocomoco was situated high on the sandy bluffs rising above the north side of the Pamunkey River (a tributary of today's York River) in what is now Gloucester County, Virginia.

Then known by the Native American name *Tsenacomoco*, Virginia's Tidewater region is where freshwater rivers meet the salty Atlantic Ocean. In Pocahontas's day, food sources were plentiful on land and sea. Paddling canoes that had been dug out of tree trunks, Native Americans gathered mussels and oysters from the rich local waters. Traps, spears, nets, and lines with hooks made of bone were used to catch fish. For larger fish—such as the great sturgeon, which might reach fourteen feet in length—bows with cords attached to the arrows made fishing easier. On land, in

Canoe Construction

In an area interlaced with waterways, canoes were the primary means of transportation for most Native Americans living in the Tidewater region. Called *quintans*, the largest of these watercrafts could extend some fifty feet, have a depth of four feet, and hold forty men along with their gear. The average canoe, though, usually held anywhere from ten to thirty people. Each canoe was made from a single tree—usually cypress, but pine and chestnut were also used depending on availability and access.

After a tree was selected in the forest, a fire was built at its base. Alternately burning and chipping away at the charred wood eventually felled the tree. Once it was on the ground, small fires and red-hot stones were used to burn down the wood along a center line. Care was always taken to make sure the fire did not spread to the sides of the log, which might also be covered with a paste of wet mud for added protection. As the wood along the center burned, shells or stone tools were used to carefully scrape out the charred bits. Eventually a canoe was formed with straight sides and a flat bottom. The flat-bottomed design meant that the canoe could either be paddled from a sitting position, or poled by standing upright.

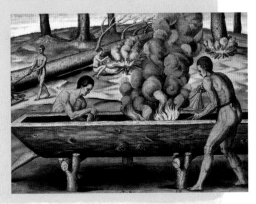

Carefully burning and scraping, two native craftsmen use simple tools to construct a dugout canoe from the trunk of a massive tree.

Native Americans paddle their dugout canoe through waters teeming with sea life in this 16th-century engraving by Englishman John White.

the forests filled with tall trees, hunters carrying bows and arrows wrapped themselves in deerskins and imitated animal movements to get closer to wild game including rabbits, beavers, opossums, wild turkeys, and squirrels.

Life along the Chesapeake

In addition to fishing and hunting, Native Americans who lived along the shores of *Tschiswapeki* (the "great shellfish bay" that today is known as the Chesapeake) gathered roots, berries, and nuts for food. Members of the Powhatan nation were also excellent farmers. Families worked together to prepare individual gardens. First, trees and brush were cleared, and then seeds were planted. Women were responsible for weeding and tending the gardens, while the children shooed away birds and small animals that might try to eat sprouting seedlings, a job Pocahontas would have had. Corn, a diet staple, was planted once a month in April, May, and June. This staggered schedule guaranteed ripening corn well into the fall months. Sown amidst the rows of corn were squash and beans. Together, all three crops ensured a bountiful harvest that could also be smoked or dried to supplement a family's diet during winter months, when fresh game might be scarce.

Before the arrival of Europeans, the Powhatan people had little metal, but they were quick to put locally found resources to use for a variety of functions. Tools such as knives, axes, drills, and arrows were made with wood and stone, while antlers and large bones from deer and other wild game were formed into needles, primitive drills, fish hooks, and other useful items. Clay, bark, animal skin, and turtle shells were made into cups, bowls, or storage containers for food. Pocahontas's people used the land and its rich resources wisely, and appreciated the bounty it offered them.

Working together in the fields, Native Americans planted crops that could be dried and stored. Staggered planting schedules helped ensure a longer growing season.

CHAPTER 2

The Child Matoaka

A child of [ten years] old; which, not only for feature, countenance, and proportion, much [exceeds] any of the rest of [Powhatan's] people . . .
—John Smith

Although likely separated from her mother at a fairly young age, Pocahontas was probably pampered and well cared for by her father's numerous other wives. Like many Native Americans, Powhatan mothers carried their infants strapped into cradleboards tied to their backs. Pocahontas, too, would have very likely been toted around in the same

manner by her mother or other women of the tribe. Once they were walking, most young Powhatan children participated in various running games and sometimes dressed up like their parents—wearing necklaces of beads or shells and painting their bodies with various designs.

Wrapping their precious cargo in soft animal skins, Powhatan women carried their infants in cradleboards similar to the one shown in this latter-day photograph.

Clothing for the members of the Tidewater tribes was simple, and little was worn except in the colder months. Deerskin was used to make leather robes, moccasins, and leggings that provided added warmth in the winter. In addition, turkey feathers were sewn together to make mantles, or short capes, that also offered protection from colder temperatures. During the rest of the year, most men and women wore a basic breechcloth—a piece of clothing resembling an apron that hung from around the waist—though some women wore a type of fringed skirt as well. *A Briefe and True Report of The New Found Land of Virginia,* written by Thomas Hariot and published in 1590, described "people clothed with loose mantles made of [deer] skins & aprons of the same [around] their middles." The rest of their bodies remained bare.

Hairstyles varied according to social status, gender, and age. The youngest girls wore their hair cut very short on the sides and in the front, but long in the back. A married woman's hair was worn long and kept braided. Men kept their hair long and uncut on one side, but the other side was trimmed very close or shaved (using a sharpened clam shell). This prevented their hair from getting tangled in their bowstrings when hunting. No elaborate head gear was worn—such as the enormous feathered bonnets donned by Plains Indians—but hair ornaments might include feathers or a rattlesnake's rattle. Both men and women hung chains, beads, or other objects from holes in their ears. One Jamestown colonist wrote of natives who sported rat skins and live snakes attached to their earlobes. Intricate tattoos and painted designs were common body ornaments. Colorful depictions of snakes, birds, flowers, and various woodland creatures were created by mixing tinted powders with oil. Bloodroot—a plant which produces a deep red shade—was a popular choice.

Tribesmen in simple breechcloths—their bodies intricately painted—grace the cover of an early European guide to the new colony of Virginia.

A Rich Land

All Powhatan villages were located near some source of water, as native peoples depended on rivers and bays for food, drinking water, and transportation routes. Women were as equally skilled as men at canoeing. Other than canoeing, the only other method of transportation was walking. There were no horses, wagons, or roads. Narrow pine- and leaf-carpeted trails, originally made by animals and no greater than about twenty inches in width, were the primary transportation routes used by the Powhatan Indians as they traveled through forested areas. No doubt Pocahontas and her friends silently walked these same trails as they explored the woods around their village.

Native Americans living in the Tidewater region got almost everything they needed from the richness of the land. Food, materials for building, and basic utensils were all readily available nearby. However, items such as pearls, copper, certain types of shells or beads, and any other luxury goods could only be obtained via trade. An extensive network of commerce extended as far away as the Great Lakes region. For many Native Americans, the only appeal of the strangers who arrived from Europe was in the unusual and never-before-seen objects they had available for trade.

No doubt Pocahontas and her friends silently walked these same trails as they explored the woods around their village.

Ritual and celebration were an important part of Powhatan life. Pocahontas probably joined her elders during feasts and dancing. Songs and dances were incorporated into a variety of occasions and events, including happy celebrations, grieving rituals, and preparations for war. Music was performed by beating drums, blowing through reeds, and by rattling seeds inside dried gourds.

Childhood Days

Pocahontas—like others of her tribe—probably learned to swim when she was quite young. All tribe members—men, women, and children—took ritual baths in the river at sunrise and sunset. The youngest children, who had not yet learned to swim, were carried into the river on adults' shoulders. In addition to swimming and playing, Pocahontas and other native children of the Eastern Woodlands were taught simple practical skills from an early age. It was important that they learn to become contributing members of the community.

Boys practiced fishing skills and were shown how to hunt with small bows by older males in the community. Young girls were instructed by their mothers and other women in the tribe

Games and sports were popular among Native Americans of the Virginia Tidewater region. Here, young men practice their bow skills, race, and toss balls at a basketlike target.

about their responsibilities. These included gathering wood; planting and tending gardens; making clay pottery, which would be used for cooking and storage; weaving baskets of wicker, hemp, or grass; curing hides; crafting beadwork (known as wampum) from bits of shell; fashioning clothing from animal skins; and watching over very young children.

Cooking was also a very important task undertaken by women. Outdoor fire pits held spits that were used to smoke or roast wild turkey or duck. Large clay pots held stews and soups of corn and other vegetables, while corncakes and bread were baked in the ashes of the cooking fire. Many of the English settlers that later came to the area remarked that the Powhatan women were seldom idle.

Wampum

Powhatan Indians, as well as other Native Americans in the East, used purple and white beads made of shell to craft wampum. Similar to European tapestries or Scottish plaids, the designs, patterns, and pictures that were formed often told a story or the history of a family. Wampum might be used for currency, to celebrate a great event, or as elaborate clothing decoration.

Small pieces of shell were hollowed to form tube-like beads. Using a primitive drill-like tool, first one side of the shell piece and then the other was carefully pierced. Then bits of sandstone or other mildly abrasive materials were used to smooth and form curved shapes. Each bead was then threaded onto a leather thong or a string made of plant fiber. Whelk (large sea snails) and clamshells were popular choices for bead-making. Europeans later brought glass beads made in Venice across the Atlantic to use in trade with Native Americans. The beads' unusual blue color was highly prized by the Powhatan Indians. John Smith wrote that the great chief himself was especially interested in the Venetian beads and, on at least one occasion, traded two or three hundred bushels of corn for a small quantity of blue beads.

Bits of shell were hand-drilled and carefully strung to create wampum belts such as this early 19th-century example from another Eastern Woodlands tribe, the Iroquois.

Due to her position as the favored daughter of the great chief Powhatan, Pocahontas was probably spared from performing many of the tasks that most women and young girls of lesser status took on as part of their daily routines. Her position of privilege within the community set her apart. Adulthood came early, though, for all Powhatan peoples, and marriages usually took place between the ages of thirteen and fifteen.

While children did mature quite early and take on more responsibilities of adulthood at a younger age than today, Powhatan youngsters were still closely supervised and watched over. Despite early English settlers' reports to the contrary, Powhatan children did not run wild. Even though various English ships had visited the Tidewater region as early as the 1580s and reports came in about the strangers in the area, Pocahontas in all likelihood would have remained behind in her village—safe and protected with other children her age. In fact, Pocahontas probably did not see her first white man until the 1607 arrival of the Jamestown settlers. But it is with the appearance of these settlers that the story of Pocahontas truly begins.

The First Europeans

Before the arrival of the Jamestown settlers, Tidewater natives' interaction with Europeans had been brief, disturbing, and primarily limited to contact with the Spanish—who had kidnapped a local boy during a 1560 raid. Arriving in the Tidewater area several years later, Catholic Jesuit priests had attempted to establish a small settlement near the mouth of today's James River. When members of local tribes destroyed the site in 1571, the Spanish brutally retaliated by killing some forty locals, including seven Indians who were hung from a ship's rigging in full view of those on shore. Although the Spanish

Acting on behalf of Queen Elizabeth I, Sir Walter Raleigh (c. 1554–1618) dispatched the first English settlers to set up a colony on the Mid-Atlantic shore.

ceased their attempts to colonize the area, local tribes were left with a taste of revenge unsatisfied.

England, despite a few early colonization efforts, had had little luck on North America's eastern coast. Two of the most well-known failures were sponsored by Sir Walter Raleigh in the late sixteenth century. Although Raleigh himself never set foot on North American soil, he encouraged its colonization. One group that settled on what is now North Carolina's Outer Banks became known as the "Lost Colony" after all members vanished without a trace.

Much of what is known today about the Tidewater natives' history and way of life comes from the writings of early European settlers in the region. While the details reported by Englishmen such as John Smith and William Strachey are of great historical value, it is important to remember that the early colonists viewed local natives as savages whose culture was very primitive. Therefore, most of the writings and reports about Pocahontas and her kinsmen are colored by the settlers' own worldview. The experiences and interactions they had with local tribes probably reflect some issues and events that were misinterpreted or misunderstood.

The Lost Colony

Perhaps the most famous of England's failed attempts to colonize the Eastern Seaboard, Roanoke Island and the mystery of what happened there remains among the most historically compelling. Organized by the English explorer and adventurer Sir Walter Raleigh in 1587, a group of 150 men, women, and children sailed across the Atlantic that May to establish a settlement in the Chesapeake Bay region. After making landfall at Roanoke Island (off the coast of present-day North Carolina), the decision was made to settle there instead, in the remains of an earlier encampment.

Seemingly friendly overtures from local Croatoan Indians calmed the settlers' fears about possible attacks, and the small colony appeared to thrive. That August marked the birth of Virginia Dare, the first child of English ancestry to be born in the New World. Not long afterward, the colony's governor (and Virginia Dare's grandfather), John White, sailed back to England for supplies with the promise of a speedy return. But political turmoil in Europe, combined with mishaps at sea, brought a three-year delay. When White finally did return, the colony had been abandoned and no trace was ever found of its settlers.

This 19th-century engraving depicts the baptism of Virginia Dare, the first English child born on North American soil. Her fate—and that of the Lost Colony—remains a mystery.

CHAPTER 3

From Across the Sea

. . . the winds continued contrary for so long that
we were forced to stay there some time, where we
suffered great storms, but by the skillfulness of the
Captain we suffered no great loss or danger.

—George Percy, writing of the Jamestown settlers'
departure from England

On December 19 and 20, 1606, one hundred men and four boys gathered in Blackwell, England, just down river on the Thames from the center of London. Here they boarded three ships—the *Susan Constant*, the *Godspeed*, and the *Discovery*—for a voyage across the Atlantic that was expected to last five weeks. These future colonists, as directed by officers of the Virginia Company, a British trading group that sponsored the endeavor, were being sent to establish a settlement in the New World. Their hopes for success were high.

Loaded on the three ships were five months' worth of provisions, assumed to be more than enough for the first months of the new settlement's existence. Included were grain, hogs, salted pork and beef, and various articles of defense—among them lances, helmets, muskets, cannons, armor, and metal pellets for use as ammunition. They also took along a shallop, a small boat, packed aboard in pieces that could be easily assembled and used for exploration in areas where the larger ships would not be able to travel.

Shown is a 20th-century print of the *Susan Constant*, the *Godspeed*, and the *Discovery*. Departing England for the New World, passengers had no idea what awaited them in Virginia.

Finally, a sealed box was placed on each ship—not to be opened until their arrival in Virginia. Contained inside were instructions regarding the new colony and the names of those who had been chosen to serve as its leaders once ashore.

One month later, hampered by poor weather conditions, the three ships still sat at anchor within sight of the English coastline. Morale was extremely low, and tempers were short. Several of the wealthier passengers onboard had grown tired of waiting and were ready to abandon the voyage. It was only the intervention of Reverend Robert Hunt—who was to serve as chaplain for the new settlement—that kept the plans on course. Even though horribly seasick, Hunt appealed to those who wished to end the mission. If Hunt would not consider turning back in his condition, how could they? Not long afterward, the weather improved and the journey began.

Shallops

Small, well constructed, and relatively easy to assemble, these lightweight open workboats were important tools for settlers arriving in the New World. Designed primarily for use on rivers or along the coastline, shallops could be rowed, sailed, or propelled through the water using a combination of both oars and sails. Each boat typically had one or two masts, at least one sail, and held six to eight pairs of oars. They were used to transport people or goods from one point to another, for mapping or surveying expeditions, and in trading ventures with local Indians. Shallops ranged in size from twenty-five to forty-five feet long, were designed to hold about two dozen men, and could carry several days' worth of food and supplies.

Photographed dockside, this modern-day shallop replica was constructed in Plymouth, Massachusetts.

Built in Europe, disassembled, and stowed aboard one of the ships for the Atlantic voyage, the shallop used by John Smith and the first Jamestown colonists was hoisted onto the Virginia shore and assembled in just two days. In later years, shallops were used as fishing boats in North American coastal waters.

Reverend Robert Hunt (c. 1568–1608) and other Jamestown colonists give thanks at Cape Henry, their first landing site in Virginia.

Crossing the Atlantic

Hoping to form a small model of English society in the new colony, the ships' rosters included—in addition to the chaplain—soldiers, bricklayers, carpenters, laborers, a tailor, a barber, a surgeon, and some two dozen passengers simply listed as "gentlemen." Captaining the *Susan Constant* was Christopher Newport, an experienced sea veteran. Also aboard was John Smith, a soldier and explorer who would play an important role in establishing relations with the native peoples of Virginia.

After just a short time at sea, it became apparent to all that the conditions were extremely cramped. At 116 feet in length, the 120-ton *Susan Constant* was the largest vessel. Between colonists and crew, she carried seventy-one onboard. The forty-ton *Godspeed* was about sixty-eight feet long and carried fifty-two onboard. The twenty-ton *Discovery*, about fifty feet in length, had a total of twenty-one passengers and crew.

While these dimensions may *seem* large, actual deck space was limited by the ships' designs. Each had originally been built to carry cargo, not passengers. In terms of usable space, the *Godspeed*'s area would be equivalent to about three parking spaces today. Although a few cabins had been hastily built before departure for some of the more wealthy passengers, on each ship most travelers slept in hammocks or on straw mattresses placed on the decks. A reenactment voyage from England to Jamestown made in 1985 on a replica of the *Godspeed* had only fourteen onboard instead of the original fifty-two. One of the modern-day sailors noted that even just fourteen people created a crowd on the ship. He speculated that, by comparison, fifty-two people would have meant an extremely cramped living situation

Looking at a map today, a fairly straight course across the Atlantic traveling in a

Also aboard was John Smith, . . . who would play an important role in establishing relations with the native peoples of Virginia.

southwesterly direction would seem the fastest way for the three ships to reach Virginia. However, navigation in the early seventeenth century was still primitive. Making use of the Atlantic's **trade winds** was really the simplest route across the great ocean, and the one with which most captains were familiar. Captain Newport predictably followed the southern trade winds first to France's Brittany coast. From there, it was on to Spain and southwest to the Canary Islands for a brief stop to take in fresh water. After successfully crossing the vast Atlantic and reaching the West Indies, it was reasoned, the three ships could work their way northward using a compass—the only reasonably accurate

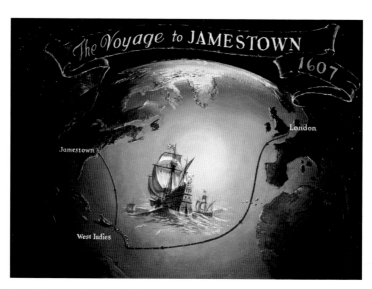

Dependent on trade winds and limited navigational aids, the Jamestown fleet followed a southwesterly course before crossing the vast Atlantic and arriving safely in the West Indies. The ships then sailed north to reach the eastern coastline of the New World.

navigation tool onboard most ships of the day. In addition to limited navigation tools, there was no reliable method of measuring speed or time. Also, contact between the three ships was difficult at best—especially at night. These shortcomings became more and more apparent as seemingly endless days, weeks, and then months passed.

To add further to the problems on the voyage, tempers had flared soon after the ships left the Canary Islands. An argument between John Smith and Edward Maria Wingfield, a wealthy merchant and fellow passenger, had intensified to the point that Smith was charged with plotting an onboard rebellion. He was put in leg irons (metal bands that restricted movement), and confined to the brig—the ship's jail—for the remainder of the voyage. Even though many felt that Smith had been falsely accused, the punishment for such charges was death. He would remain confined until a later opportunity when he could be brought onshore and hanged.

A New Land

Finally, in the early hours of April 26, 1607—more than four months since the travelers had first sailed out on the Thames—they spotted the Virginia shoreline. Entering the Chesapeake Bay, the three ships dropped anchor.

Captain Newport, accompanied by some thirty men, rowed ashore while John Smith spied his first glimpse of the new land as a condemned man locked in the brig. Springtime in Virginia seemed to hold the promise of riches to come, especially after

After months at sea, the Jamestown colonists first glimpsed the Virginia shoreline on April 26, 1607. Once ashore, the Englishmen were watched by Powhatan tribesmen concealed in the nearby forest.

the cramped conditions of the long voyage. Staying ashore all afternoon and into the early evening, Newport and his party headed back to the beach as darkness fell.

Unaware that they were being watched, the party had a surprise waiting for them in the dusky darkness of the Virginia shoreline. As an eyewitness later recalled, "there came the savages creeping upon all fours from the hills like bears, with their bows in their mouths, [who] charged us very desperately." Even though two men in Newport's party were injured in the attack, the English returned fire with their muskets and were able to get back to their ships.

Following their pre-departure instructions, Christopher Newport opened the sealed boxes. He then announced the names of those who had been selected to serve as council members and govern the new colony. Among those chosen was the name of John Smith, thereby granting him the equivalent of a get-out-of-jail-free card. Even though this news was good for Smith, he was probably not too happy to learn that Edward Wingfield, the man with whom he had so violently quarreled, had been named head of the new colony.

First president of the Jamestown colony, Edward Maria Wingfield (c. 1550–1630), had initially called for John Smith's execution.

After several days of exploration along the Virginia coastline, on May 13, the three ships reached what would become known as Jamestown Island (after James I, the English king since 1603). As another indication

The Virginia Company

Also known as the London Company, the Virginia Company was a commercial trading corporation founded in April of 1606. A **charter** granted by England's King James I authorized the company to conduct business in the New World between the latitudes of 34° and 41°—a stretch of coastline extending some 450 miles south from today's Philadelphia, Pennsylvania, to Cape Fear, North Carolina. Its aims were lofty ones—to search for gold, locate a trade route through to the Pacific Ocean and the Far East, ship local raw materials and goods manufactured onsite in the New World back to England for sale and distribution, and convert native peoples to Christianity.

The company's influence was extensive. It had the power to appoint the local governing authority and other officials. It was also responsible for providing transportation and supplies for new settlers. Initial support for the Virginia Company was strong, but nearly nonexistent profits combined with a high death rate among new settlers eventually brought discontent. Even though the company was dissolved in 1624, Virginia then became a royal colony. More than a century later, it would become one of the original thirteen colonies that made up the new United States of America.

Printed two years after the first settlers arrived in Jamestown, this Virginia Company pamphlet encouraged others to settle and invest in the New World colony.

Honoring their monarch, King James I (1566–1625), the English colonists gave his name to their new settlement and the deep river running along its shoreline.

of their loyalty to their monarch, the men also named the water lapping the island's shores the James River.

The choice of a settlement location had been clearly defined by officials from the Virginia Company. The site should not be one already occupied by any local natives, and this location appeared to be vacant. It also looked as though it would be fairly easy to defend against attack by sea or land—another requirement of the Virginia Company. In fact, the "island" was actually a **peninsula** that was naturally hidden by a bend in the river and accessed from the mainland via a narrow neck of land. At the river bend, a deep channel cut by the river's current ran so close to shore that large ships could be tied up to trees, rather than anchored in the river. A high point on the peninsula also appeared to be an excellent site for a fort. Disregarding the lack of freshwater and acres of mosquito-infested marsh—two important points that would later cause the colonists a great deal of misery—the location seemed, according to John Smith, "a very fit place for the erecting of a great [city]." Finally, on May 14, 1607, nearly five months after departing England for an anticipated voyage of only five weeks, the colonists came ashore onto Jamestown Island to gaze at their future home.

On May 14, 1607, the colonists finally landed at the site they would name Jamestown. Their arrival would bring changes Pocahontas and her people could not imagine.

CHAPTER 4

Jamestown

*Heaven and earth never agreed better to frame
a place for man's habitation. . . .*
—*John Smith*

That their initial welcome from area natives had not
exactly been friendly seemed not to discourage the
English colonists. By this point, they were all probably so
relieved to be off the three ships that just about anything
would have seemed like paradise.

In truth, the 1,600-acre site of Jamestown Island was
not the best choice. Even though it did not *appear* to be
occupied by natives, the colonists were unaware that the
site sat smack in the middle of the great kingdom of
Powhatan—and, more specifically—on tribal hunting
grounds. Huge trees
and vines as thick as
a man's thigh had to
be cleared before a
settlement could
be constructed.

One of the colonists' first
tasks in Jamestown was to
clear trees and begin
building. Houses were
grouped inside a triangular,
wood-sided fort that
offered some protection
from Indian attack.

Soon, the pleasantly warm breezes of spring gave way to the scorching heat and humidity of summer and then to ice-cold winter winds that blew across the marshlands. Good drinking water was scarce—much of the nearby water was **contaminated** or affected by seeping saltwater from the James River. Contaminated water brought with it illness and fever and, eventually, the deaths of many of the colonists. But few of these future hazards were considered when the site was chosen.

Work Begins

After a few arguments as to the site's suitability, a final decision was made to stay. "Now [it falls to] every man to work," wrote John Smith. "Cut down trees . . . pitch tents . . . some make gardens, some nets. . . ." Soldiers set off to scout out the area, laborers began clearing underbrush, a makeshift chapel was erected using a ship's sail, and a defensive wall made of brush

Watching silently from the nearby forest, native tribesmen gave regular reports of the Jamestown settlers' activities to Pocahontas's father, Chief Powhatan.

was set up. In addition, a military guard was put in place to watch for any trouble.

For the Native American residents, the response to the Englishmen's arrival was probably mixed—a blend of curiosity, hostility, fear, and fascination. But if anything was to be done, the decision rested firmly with Powhatan. Just a few days later, on May 18, a local chief arrived accompanied by one hundred armed warriors. This show of force was impressive, and made the intended point—that the English colonists were clearly outnumbered. Despite initially friendly overtures, the meeting did not end well. A scuffle broke out between a soldier and an Indian over a missing hatchet. However, two days later, forty more warriors arrived toting a deer carcass that was meant as a peace offering.

Before the two groups parted company, a mutual display of weaponry skills using leather and metal targets took place that was no doubt intended to both impress and intimidate participants on each side. In one display, an Indian arrow penetrated a metal shield that had been set up as a target—greatly impressing the Europeans. These displays were understandably confusing to the English settlers. One minute the Indians might appear friendly and welcoming, but the next encounter might be a hostile one.

Preserved through the centuries, Powhatan's deerskin mantle is adorned with shell decorations that were believed to symbolize the balance of power throughout the lands governed by the mighty chief.

Prior to the arrival of the English in Jamestown, Powhatan had initially inherited the leadership of some six to eight tribes from his father. Over a period of thirty years, he had incorporated some thirty different groups into an empire that also bore his name. Like the Appomatoc, Mattaponi, Arrohatoc, and Pamunkey, many tribes in the Powhatan nation took their name from local rivers. Each tribe within this vast network had its own unique customs and traditions as well as a separate *werowance*, or chief, but Powhatan was ruler over all. Although lacking an elaborate, multilayered political organization (such as that of the Iroquois Confederacy to the north), the Powhatan nation was well structured. Its trade and peacekeeping policies functioned smoothly and provided sufficiently for the needs of the people.

Shown perched above his tribesmen in this engraving from John Smith's history of Virginia, Chief Powhatan ruled a kingdom that stretched some 8,000 square miles throughout the mid-Atlantic region.

Although all tribes in this area were united under Powhatan's rule, it took some time before the English settlers began to realize that they were dealing with an assortment of different Indian groups whose reactions to, and opinions of, Europeans varied. Overall, it seems that the English viewed the locals as prone to thievery, irregular in temperament, and possessing a childlike curiosity.

Since friendly encounters seemed to outnumber hostile actions, all seemed to be well. That assumption was put to rest a week later, however, when about two hundred warriors from yet another Powhatan nation tribe—one led by Powhatan's brother, Opechancanough—descended on the settlement in a full-scale attack that lasted about an hour. Unimpressed after a meeting with Captain Newport, Opechancanough had evidently taken it upon himself to rid the Powhatan world of the English settlers.

The colonists, most of their arms still packed away, had been out planting corn and were forced to run for cover. Indians, wrote Smith, "came up almost into the fort, shot through the tents." Finally, a lucky blast from the ship's

Never as tolerant of the English as Powhatan, the chief's brother Opechancanough (center) often spoke out against foreign settlement to fellow tribesmen.

cannon struck a huge branch, which crashed into the attackers' midst. Alarmed by the noise, the Indians quickly retreated. Around a dozen of the colonists were wounded and one boy was

This contemporary model depicts the triangular-shaped Jamestown fort, showing its defensive position on a peninsula above the James River.

killed. Even though an arrow passed directly through Edward Wingfield's beard, he was miraculously unhurt. This incident convinced one and all that the construction of a fort should be a top priority. All able-bodied colonists worked around the clock building a wooden palisade defensive structure shaped like a triangle that enclosed about an acre of land.

Friend or Foe?

Meanwhile, reports were filtering back to Powhatan—including, no doubt, the news of his brother's unsuccessful challenge of the colonists. In all likelihood, Pocahontas had also heard of the new arrivals with their clothing made of metal (armor) and sunburned necks and faces. Now about age twelve, Pocahontas was—in the custom of her culture—on the edge of adulthood. As the favored daughter of her people's most important ruler, Pocahontas's thoughts might have echoed those of her father: What was the strangers' purpose in coming here? How long would they remain? Were they friend or foe? Should they be trusted? Watched? Destroyed?

On June 22, Captain Newport and his crew left the settlers behind and sailed out of the James River on two of the ships—the *Susan Constant* and the *Godspeed*. They were bound for England, with a promise to return within twenty weeks. The fort, such as it was, had been completed, and additional supplies were needed. The report he carried with him for the Virginia Company seemed optimistic—"within less than seven weeks, we are fortified well against the Indians. We have sown [a] good store of wheat . . . we have built some houses . . . and still as God shall enable us with strength we will better and better our proceedings." Although conditions were hard, it was in the colonists' best interest to paint a rosy picture for the folks back home. Without additional support—and much-needed supplies—the future of the new settlement of Jamestown was uncertain.

During Newport's absence, activity at the fort seemed to grind to a halt. A number of the "gentlemen" seemed content to simply wait for the supply ships from England to return, while Smith and others continued to focus on the settlement's most pressing need—food. Those who remained idle seemed to believe, unwisely, that Captain Newport would arrive right on schedule as promised—sometime in November. After their own experience on the Atlantic crossing—where a trip expected to take five weeks lasted nearly five months—it is hard to understand how they could be so unrealistic.

Disgusted by his fellow colonists' lack of initiative, Smith wrote "they would rather starve and rot with idleness, [than] be persuaded to do anything for their own relief without constraint."

Christopher Newport (c. 1560–1617)

Unlike other well-known sea captains of the day, Christopher Newport was a commoner with little formal education. However, his reputation as a top-notch navigator, fair but stern captain, and strong leader of his men, along with his commitment to the colonizing efforts of the British Empire, won him the respect of prominent members of the business and military communities.

Early in his naval career, Newport had participated in the defeat of the Spanish Armada by Great Britain. Later, while a highly successful **privateer** in the West Indies for Queen Elizabeth I, he lost his right arm in a fierce battle off the coast of Cuba. Between 1606 and 1611, Newport made five trips to the New World from England, transporting valuable supplies and additional settlers. In his later years, he led several lengthy trading voyages for the British East India Company and transported the first British ambassadors to parts of Persia, in modern-day Iran, and India.

Leader of the three-ship fleet that brought the first settlers to Jamestown, Christopher Newport was an experienced ship's captain and successful privateer.

In the meantime, daily **rations** soon dropped to a half pint of barley boiled in water along with an equal portion of wheat. Both were worm-infested. The lack of fresh drinking water soon became a definite problem. Since no well had been dug or spring water found on the mainland, the colonists were forced to draw water from the river, which was used for both drinking and bathing. As the summer went on, the river water became more brackish (salty). Low tide made things even worse as the water was full of slime and filth. Clothes soiled with human waste were also washed in the same river, causing disease among the settlers.

Without additional support—and much-needed supplies—the future of the new settlement of Jamestown was uncertain.

Lack of food, unsanitary conditions, and sickness began to take their toll. At times, no more than five colonists were strong enough to stand guard against attack. Nearly everyone suffered—even John Smith fell ill. But Edward Wingfield remained suspiciously healthy. Eventually, it was discovered that Wingfield had a secret stash of concealed goods that included beef, wine, eggs, and oatmeal. Not long after his deceit was revealed, Wingfield's term as president ended abruptly when the remaining original council members voted him out of office. But by mid-August, nearly half of the colony was dead.

A Change of Fortune

Despite the fact that Powhatan was, in all likelihood, receiving frequent reports from his tribesmen living in the Jamestown area of conditions at the English fort, he made no move to attack. Why the great chief did not choose to simply wipe out the few remaining colonists remains unknown. He may have assumed that the colony would simply die out on its own and that there was no point in wasting his energy by hastening the end of Jamestown.

This decision not to attack may have been a grave tactical error. Had Powhatan elected to converge on Jamestown and kill the settlers, England's colonizing plans for the area would have suffered a huge setback. Instead, Powhatan elected to begin a steady pattern of trading. The corn and other provisions that the chief's people brought to the settlement were exchanged for tools, beads, and other European goods. There is no clear reason why Powhatan chose to do this. After all, had he done nothing, in the hopes that the settlement would die out, any of the colonists' remaining tools and supplies would have been his for the taking. But because of this food trade, the Jamestown settlers began to strengthen and recover.

Steady trade with the Indians brought much-needed supplies to the Jamestown fort. In this latter-day illustration, John Smith offers an exchange of tools for food.

CHAPTER 5

Smith's Capture

At last they brought him to Werowocomoco, where was Powhatan, their Emperor.

—*John Smith*

Now that conditions seemed to be improving at the Jamestown settlement, John Smith began extensive explorations of the surrounding area. Keeping in mind at least two of the original directives of the Virginia Company—to search for a route to the Pacific and to look for gold—he set out on several excursions with small parties of men from the fort. As Smith traveled, he drew carefully detailed maps with information about the area and gave English names to new locations he encountered.

With his military experience, Smith had learned the importance of speaking the local language and—through his travels in the areas surrounding Jamestown—had begun to understand certain Algonquian words. *Mockasins* were shoes; *pokatawer* meant fire. Enemies were *marrapough*; friends were *netoppew*, and good friends were *wingapoh*. In his meetings with various natives during his travels, he was careful to study the rituals of their daily lives—how the men hunted and the women planted, harvested, and cooked the food. The women, Smith also observed, "love children very dearly." Bartering with the Indians for food or other trade goods, Smith gradually earned a modest degree

In addition to his writings about Virginia, John Smith also produced this map giving the New England region its name in 1614.

of respect from many of the native people he encountered. Known as a man of his word, Smith was generally perceived by locals as tough but fair.

In December of 1607, Smith, a party of Englishmen from the fort, and two Indian guides set out in the shallop to explore a tributary of the James River called the Chickahominy. As Smith and his party traveled about fifty miles upriver, he observed the plentiful fish and waterfowl, the vast planted fields, and the many Indian settlements.

Eventually, the shallop reached a spot where the river became quite narrow and the current much faster. Fearing damage to his vessel, Smith opted to canoe upriver with two

John Smith (c. 1580–1631)

Leaving his English home in his mid-teens following the death of his father, John Smith began his military career shortly thereafter. Serving as a **mercenary** in Europe while in his twenties, he was wounded, captured, and sold as a slave. He was able to escape by reportedly murdering his harsh Turkish master. Following his return to England, Smith became involved in plans to set up the new North American colony of Virginia. He arrived there with the original group of settlers in 1607. Smith served on the colony's governing council and later as its president. Two years later, a gunpowder-burn injury forced him to return to England. He traveled back across the Atlantic only once more when, in 1614, he sailed northward to an area between Maine and Cape Cod. Carefully mapping the area, he named it New England.

Never married, Smith wrote a number of books about his travels and the British colonization efforts in North America. Despite some criticisms regarding the accuracy of his writings, Smith detailed accounts of the colonization of Jamestown and offered valuable insight into the traditions of Powhatan society.

Portrayed here with armor and sword, John Smith's name will be forever associated with the Jamestown settlement and the Powhatan princess, Pocahontas.

of his men and the native guides. His orders to the others were to remain onboard the shallop at all times until he returned. Two miles upriver, Smith and his small party paddled to shore. Leaving one guide behind with his two men, Smith and the other guide set off on foot to explore the area. The decision to divide the group into three parts would prove a fatal one for some members of Smith's party.

Under Attack

Disregarding Smith's orders, the original group remaining with the shallop came ashore. They were quickly attacked by natives waiting in the brush. All but one of the men made it safely back to the boat. The straggler—a laborer named George Cassen—was horribly tortured and then killed. The two men who had canoed upriver with Smith also met a similar fate. Finally, Smith himself—belatedly realizing that he and his party had been ambushed—came under attack. Surrounded by what looked like an army of hostile Indians, Smith grabbed his guide to use as a human shield. Despite this precaution, Smith was hit in the thigh with an arrow. Luckily, the thickness of his winter clothing saved him and he received just a grazing wound.

While the loudness of Smith's weapon probably gave him a momentary advantage, he was clearly in a difficult position. Following a backward course toward the river, which was, perhaps, his one hope of safety, Smith lost his footing and fell into a mucky swamp. Unable to hold onto his pistol and pull himself out of the ooze, he threw his weapon down in disgust and gave himself up.

Quick thinking, though, kept Smith from suffering the same fate as his fellow explorers. Pulling a compass from his coat pocket, Smith displayed it to his captors, among them

In this illustration from his history of Virginia, Smith is bound to a tree facing execution by armed warriors. Fortunately, the Englishman's quick thinking bought him some time.

Opechancanough, Powhatan's brother. The moving dial of the compass was curious, but the clear yet impenetrable glass was truly amazing. Thinking Smith held a magical object with special powers, the Indians wondered if Smith was himself a great chief. Perhaps it would be better not to kill him, but to take him to Powhatan.

For the next several weeks, Smith and his captors followed a roundabout path, passing through many of the villages that made up Powhatan's realm. As the group traveled, word spread

After displaying a glass-topped compass to his captors, John Smith was saved from being killed. Unsure whether he had magical powers, the tribesmen took Smith to Powhatan.

of Smith's capture and his possible status as some sort of magical chief. At each settlement, crowds lined up to see this stocky, bear-like man with his matted hair and beard, dressed in odd clothes that included a vest of armor. For many of the Powhatan people, this was their first close-up view of one of the European strangers, and they were fascinated. No doubt Pocahontas waited with intense curiosity at her father's village for her first glimpse of this unusual man. Wined and dined at nearly every stop, Smith began to wonder if he was being fattened for some sort of cannibalistic ritual.

Powhatan's Village Camp

Finally, some time in early January, the group arrived at Powhatan's village—which most historians believe was

Werowocomoco

Extending across eight thousand square miles from what is now Virginia's Eastern Shore to Richmond, and from south of today's James River to the Potomac and beyond, Powhatan's kingdom once had its political center at Werowocomoco. Although Powhatan moved his primary residence to another location in 1609, it is likely that other tribe members remained at Werowocomoco for a number of years. How many stayed there and for exactly how long is unknown, for no historical records exist that mention the site by name after 1609.

In 1977, an archaeologist from Virginia Commonwealth University discovered Indian artifacts in plowed fields and along the beach in this area. Believing the site to be the possible location of Chief Powhatan's principal village and the probable birthplace of Pocahontas, he registered it with the Virginia Department of Historic Resources. But it was not until 2001 that serious excavations were undertaken throughout the fifty-acre site. Discoveries of native pottery, stone tools, and other evidence of Powhatan village life—such as hearth sites and soil stains (which indicate the outline of where structures were once located)—convinced a team of archaeologists that they had indeed found the long-lost Werowocomoco. Today, study of the site is ongoing.

Modern-day archaeologists carefully study the Virginia site believed to be Powhatan's headquarters at Werowocomoco.

Werowocomoco, located approximately twelve miles from Jamestown. To date, no Englishmen had ever met the great Chief Powhatan—or, if they had, none had lived to tell about the experience. But Smith, through his basic understanding of the local dialects, had heard a great deal about the natives' supreme leader—his bravery, his cunning, and his undisputed power over his tribesmen. On this day, some two hundred warriors stood in attendance glaring at Smith as though he were their fiercest enemy. Somewhere in the background, Pocahontas watched as the drama unfolded. Things did not seem to bode well for the Englishman, but he showed no fear.

Escorted into an enormous longhouse by one of the largest warriors, Smith caught his first glimpse of Powhatan, an imposing gray-headed figure of about sixty. "Before a fire upon a seat like a [bed], he sat covered with a great robe, made of raccoon [skins], and all the [tails] hanging by," wrote Smith. Necklaces made of pearls hung around the chief's neck and young women knelt by his side. With a gesture that the English captive interpreted as welcoming, Powhatan signaled for platters of food to be brought. One of his wives stepped forward with a bowl of water for Smith to wash his hands and a bundle of feathers were provided to use like a towel.

Somewhere in the background, Pocahontas watched as the drama unfolded.

Using signs and some words, Powhatan questioned Smith: Why had the English come to Powhatan's country? Speaking firmly and without fear, and using the few words he knew of Powhatan's native tongue, Smith replied that it was just a temporary stay. Captain Newport would return very soon to

Longhouses

Villages in the Tidewater region varied anywhere in size from thirty to six hundred people, with an average one hundred residents. Many villages contained at least one large, low building called a *yehakin*, or longhouse. Framed with wooden poles or saplings (young, small trees) that were then covered with woven grasses, tree bark, or animal skins, these bread-loaf shaped structures were often built to house a sizable number of people. Sometimes as many as sixty individuals—an entire clan—lived in one longhouse, which could measure 150 feet long and 20 feet wide, with a ceiling as high as 20 feet. Smaller longhouses (usually called wigwams) extended about twenty feet in length, and typically held just one family—about six people.

Inside, wooden screens and woven mats were used to divide the structure into separate living spaces. Wooden platforms or shelf-like frames lined interior walls and were used for sleeping. Shelves held equipment, tools, and food. A central fire was used for cooking during bad weather and provided warmth in cold winters. Some of the larger longhouses might even have more than one source for cooking and heating. A hole in the roof acted like a chimney, providing ventilation.

Covered by animal skins or mats of woven grasses, longhouses varied in size to accommodate a single family or an entire clan. This photograph shows a replica of a Powhatan longhouse.

take the Europeans away. (Smith did not mention the plans for settlement of the area—perhaps he sought to keep the peace with Powhatan.) If so, the chief asked, why was Smith exploring so far upriver? To look for a route to the great ocean in the west was Smith's answer. Back and forth the stately chief and the stocky Englishman conversed. Powhatan spoke of the great expanse of his chiefdom—his many tribesmen, his lands, his great riches. He then asked Smith for details about his own land, and the latter responded with descriptions of kings and queens, sailing ships and thundering cannons, scientific advancements, and strange new lands.

Taking Note of the Englishman

Among those watching and listening as Smith spun his tales was the girl Pocahontas. On the verge of young adulthood, Pocahontas probably resembled other young women of her tribe who were, in the words of one colonist, "generally beautiful, possessing an uncommon delicacy of shape and features." No doubt instilled with a sense of responsibility owing to her social ranking as the great chief's daughter, Pocahontas may have pondered the same questions her father now asked of Smith. Regardless, she apparently was intrigued by the man, his obvious lack of fear, and his answers.

Throughout his conversation with Powhatan, Smith was aware that a great fire was being lit and that a sense of anticipation was building in the room around him. Several natives who appeared to be priests or religious leaders also seemed to be chanting or calling out to their gods, while grim-faced men stood nearby with clubs in their hands. Periodically, Powhatan paused to speak to others who appeared to be advisers or lesser chiefs. It was obvious to Smith that his

Curious about the strange Englishman who did not fear her powerful father, Pocahontas later befriended Smith. She is depicted in this 20th-century engraving.

fate was being decided, and his prospects did not look good. At last, Powhatan made up his mind.

Writing of his experience in the third person seventeen years later, Smith's description is no less frightening: "a long consultation was held, but the conclusion was, two great stones were brought before Powhatan—then as many as could [lay] hands on [Smith], dragged him to them and thereon laid his head, and being ready, with their clubs, to [beat] out [his] brains. . . ."

CHAPTER 6

A Fateful Meeting

*Had the Savages not fed us, we directly [would
have] starved.*

      —*Jamestown colonist*

Held to the ground, with his head placed on two stones,
and ready to be beaten to death, John Smith could
only hope that the end would come swiftly. Suddenly,
seemingly without warning, a figure dashed into view. It
was the young Pocahontas, the chief's favorite daughter.
According to Smith, she pleaded with her father to spare
the Englishman's life, but the chief would not listen to her.
So Pocahontas took Smith's head in her arms and laid her
head over his, until Powhatan agreed that he could live.

This 19th-century illustration depicts Pocahontas saving John Smith, although
the action has been moved outside of Powhatan's longhouse. Historians
question whether the rescue was spontaneous or merely symbolic.

Nearly everyone has heard the well-known story of the Indian princess, Pocahontas, saving John Smith's life. Whether or not it happened the way Smith wrote of it—or, in fact, whether or not it really happened at all—has been endlessly debated. Why John Smith waited seventeen years to write about what took place in Powhatan's longhouse does seem strange. Some historians believe he may have exaggerated when recounting the story to make it seem more dramatic or important.

A New Look at the Story

Others think that while Smith may have truly believed he was about to be killed, the entire event was actually part of a detailed ritual performed to signify Smith's acceptance by Chief Powhatan. As a foreigner, Smith may have been forced to face his own death in order to be reborn as an adopted member of the Powhatan nation. Pocahontas's role would have then been a symbolic one—like an actor performing a part in a play. Being saved by such an important member of Powhatan's family may have signified Smith's new importance to the tribe. Regardless of what really happened, most historians do believe that this was the first time that John Smith and Pocahontas met face to face.

Ritual and **symbolism** were both very important aspects of Native American life—particularly among the Powhatan people. If, as some believe, the act of saving John Smith's life was indeed symbolic of his rebirth with respect to the tribe, the fact that Pocahontas was the one who saved him would carry even more importance.

If it was not a ritual, however, perhaps no other person could so quickly put to rest any opposition over the decision to let Smith live. While some of Powhatan's people—his brother Opechancanough among them—were highly suspicious of *any*

Although this illustration from a 20th-century advertisement depicts Pocahontas wearing a headdress more common to the Plains Indians, her status as Native American royalty is accurately implied.

European's intentions, none would dare to speak out against the actions of the chief's favorite child and such a high-ranking member of the community.

Carefully weighing his options, Powhatan probably realized that Smith might be of more value to him alive than dead and may have staged the entire experience. Regardless of whether or not the decision to save the Englishman's life was a carefully orchestrated event or the impulse of a young girl, by all accounts Pocahontas appeared to take her sponsorship role toward Smith, and later his fellow colonists, very seriously.

John Smith, Writer

Although he received little formal education, John Smith is credited with writing the first detailed account of the English colonists' settlement of America. It is unknown whether Smith originally wrote his thirteen-thousand–word text for publication or if it was simply a lengthy letter to a friend. But in the late summer of 1608, *A True Relation of Such Occurrences and Accidents of Note as Hath Happened in Virginia* was available for sale in England. Starting with the lengthy weather delay off the English coast, the book went on to chronicle the colonists' choice of settlement site, their early encounters (both friendly and unfriendly) with the natives, their initial explorations of the area, and their struggles with illness and injury. While many have questioned why no mention was made in the book about Smith's fateful first encounter with Pocahontas, it may simply be because the book was edited and published without Smith's involvement or knowledge. The editor, John Healey, even included a note explaining that some material had been intentionally removed because he thought it too personal to be included in a volume for the general public.

Soldier of fortune turned historian, John Smith is credited with writing the first detailed report of English colonization efforts in Virginia. The title page of his book is shown here.

Adopted by the Powhatan

During the next several days, while Smith remained at Werowocomoco, he lived in a small hut not far from the chief's longhouse. He and Pocahontas began to develop a friendship. Writing later of their time together, it is obvious how fond Smith became of the lively child. It was also during this brief time that they were together that Pocahontas began to learn some words of the English language. She was able to establish a basic method of communication with Smith. Both Powhatan and Pocahontas tried to make it clear to Smith that he was now considered an adopted member of the tribe. Powhatan referred to Smith as his adopted son. To Pocahontas, he was now like a brother. In addition, Smith's ranking within the tribe was that of a *werowance*, or lesser chief. Although the title was largely an honorary one, it did imply a form of allegiance to Powhatan.

Around the first of January, 1608, a fiercely painted Powhatan and several hundred of his warriors visited Smith at his hut. Spelling things out very clearly, Powhatan indicated that Smith was free to return to the English fort. However, now that he was considered a chief, he was expected to pay a tribute. The first payment Powhatan required would be a **millstone** and two cannons from the fort. Twelve of the chief's warriors would escort Smith back to Jamestown and pick up the tribute items. As Smith departed from Powhatan's headquarters on that cold January day, he knew he would see the young Indian princess again in the months to come. She would be the one to bring food that had been promised by her father to the settlers.

Arriving at Jamestown, Smith seemed more than willing to hand over the millstone and also to surrender the cannons. He gestured that the Indians were welcome to take the items and carry them back to Powhatan. Of course, the millstone was so

Although John Smith agreed to provide Powhatan with two cannons from the Jamestown fort, the guns' sizable weight made their transport back to the chief impossible. The cannon in this photograph can be found on display at Jamestown Settlement, a living history museum.

heavy that none of the warriors could move it, and since each cannon weighed in excess of three thousand pounds, Smith knew there was no way the twelve Indians would be able to haul away one, let alone two, cannons. Indicating that he had tried to grant Powhatan's initial request, Smith then offered other gifts in exchange—bells, bits of glass, beads, and copper—but no guns, not even the smaller ones. The warriors soon left the fort.

Smith's Return to Jamestown

When Smith entered the Jamestown settlement after his stay at Werowocomoco, he was shocked at what he saw. Bodies were stacked like firewood, and the smell of filth and death was obvious even in the winter's cold. Of the original 104 colonists

Trading to Survive

Once John Smith had been adopted by the Powhatan tribe, a period of fairly steady trading took place between the Jamestown colonists and the local Native Americans. While the primary item needed by the English was food, the Indians valued European manufactured goods such as glass beads, metal tools, and kettles.

Copper was as highly prized by the Powhatan Indians as gold was by the English. Like gold, the wearing or displaying of copper ornaments conveyed wealth or status in Powhatan society. The great chief himself used copper as a form of payment among his lesser chiefs. During the early seventeenth century, an ongoing war with a tribe to the west had kept the Powhatan Indians from the Great Lakes trading area—their usual source for native copper. This shortage made the copper that the Jamestown colonists had brought with them even more valuable. Knowing of its value to the Indians, colonists formed sheet copper into beads and other ornaments that were used for trading. Today, archaeologists have found thousands of sheet copper scraps throughout various excavation sites at the Jamestown settlement.

Used by the English for trading with Powhatan natives, these copper coins and scraps were found buried at the Jamestown site.

After his release from capture by Powhatan, John Smith returned to find grim conditions at the Jamestown colony. The harsh winter had taken a terrible toll on the struggling settlement.

who had sailed from England little more than a year before, fewer than forty were still alive. Starvation, illness, and Indian attacks had taken their toll.

In addition, after just barely escaping execution at the hands of Powhatan, Smith suddenly found himself condemned to hang for indirectly causing the deaths of those colonists involved in the December ambushes along the river. But like a cat with nine lives, Smith was spared once again—this time by the arrival of Christopher Newport, whose two ships brought much-needed supplies and sixty new settlers. Unfortunately, a serious fire—probably caused by improperly stored gunpowder—spread rapidly among the fort's thatched roof structures and engulfed much of the site within days of Newport's arrival. Gone were nearly all of the new supplies. "Everything my son and I had was burned," one of the newly arrived settlers wrote home, "except a mattress which had not yet been taken off the ship."

Shortly after Christopher Newport's return, a serious fire raged throughout the Jamestown settlement. Wooden structures were destroyed, as were badly needed supplies that had only just arrived from England.

Fortunately for the settlers, they were saved from further starvation by John Smith's newly formed alliance with Powhatan. Within days, food began to arrive on a pretty regular basis, and accompanying many of these deliveries was Pocahontas. The generous fare included plenty of "bread, fish, [turkeys], squirrels, [deer], and other wild beasts," wrote one colonist. The Powhatan princess took her role as a link between the people of her world and those of John Smith's very seriously. She soon became a familiar sight at the fort, as she brought messages from her father or arranged exchanges of food and trade goods.

Yet even though she took on these adult responsibilities, Pocahontas still enjoyed the lighthearted activities of childhood.

She sometimes challenged some of the boys at the fort to turn cartwheels with her. Inevitably the young lads would fall, while she was able to cartwheel effortlessly around the fort's marketplace.

Due to Pocahontas's young age, some doubt has been raised over the degree of responsibility she took on in those early years at the Jamestown settlement. Regardless, archaeological evidence such as native cooking pots and bits of turtle shell found at the site supports the theory that Indian women probably did spend a fair amount of time at Jamestown during this period. Considering her relationship with John Smith, it would make sense for Pocahontas to have accompanied others of her tribe to the fort. Writings of John Smith and other colonists also indicate that Pocahontas was a fairly frequent visitor to the settlement during this period as well.

. . . food began to arrive on a pretty regular basis, and accompanying many of these deliveries was Pocahontas.

In the months following John Smith's capture and return to Jamestown, there was a somewhat uneasy period of peace when various members of the Powhatan tribe came and went from the fort on a routine basis.

CHAPTER 7

Strained Relations

. . . I also am a king, and this is my land.

—Powhatan to the English

ollowing the fire early in 1608, things seemed to slowly improve at the Jamestown settlement. Pocahontas and her people were providing fairly steady supplies of food for the colonists to help them survive the cold winter months. Accompanied by native tribesmen, Pocahontas brought gifts of wild game—including deer carcasses slung from poles carried at the shoulder—and baskets overflowing with corn. At this point, relations between the Native Americans and the English were generally good.

The clothing worn by Pocahontas in this 19th-century engraving may not be accurate, but historians do believe she may have brought provisions to the Jamestown colonists.

What the Colonists Ate

By analyzing the contents of colonial trash dump sites, archaeologists have been able to piece together a pretty good idea of what the settlers ate. During the first two years, the colonists mainly consumed fish—such as sturgeon, which was plentiful in the James River during the summer months—and turtles. According to colonist William Strachey, there were tortoises near the entrance of their bay, but the colonists did not eat those; however, they did eat the land tortoises regularly. Other entrée choices included an assortment of native Virginian species such as raccoons, rays, oysters, and various birds such as herons and seagulls. They also ate salted pork and beef that had been brought from England.

Other than corn—which the colonists obtained via trade with the Indians—there is little evidence of any other locally grown food. Details that today's archaeologists have uncovered seem to support the writings of John Smith and his complaints about the laziness of some of the settlers. While bowling in the streets for sport was quite popular, there appears to have been little interest in planting crops during the first few years of the settlement's existence.

Sturgeon, sometimes reaching 14 feet in length, were plentiful in the waters surrounding Jamestown.

Pocahontas's efforts to preserve peace and tranquility between the two groups did not go unnoticed, and many colonists were quick to praise the Powhatan princess in later writings about this period.

Careful Negotiations

In February, Powhatan invited the Englishmen to visit him at Werowocomoco. A group of about forty men, accompanied by both John Smith and Christopher Newport, sailed to the great chief's village. Although not expecting any trouble, the Englishmen were nonetheless well armed and watchful of any possible ambush. With them they brought gifts for Powhatan—a white greyhound dog, a suit made of red wool, and a hat similar to those worn by the English **aristocracy**.

Pocahontas's efforts to preserve peace and tranquility between the two groups did not go unnoticed . . .

While the three-day meeting went well, Smith felt that Newport was not very skillful as a trader and gave in to Powhatan's demands too easily—agreeing to provide too much for too little given in return. Then, Powhatan asked the colonists to put down their arms as a friendly gesture of goodwill. All refused. Interpreting this as a lack of respect for the great chief's importance, Powhatan and his people were not pleased. Even though the meeting seemed to end on fairly good terms, a sense of uneasiness prevailed.

Despite Pocahontas's friendship with Smith and the other Englishmen, many of the Powhatan Indians began to grow suspicious about the colonists' intentions. Although historical records of this meeting do not mention the Indian princess,

Still remarkably intact, this portion of a colonial sword was unearthed by modern-day archaeologists from an early 17th-century trash pit in Jamestown.

she may well have observed the Englishmen's interactions with her father.

In April 1608, Christopher Newport set sail once again to bring back more settlers and supplies from England. Shortly before Newport's departure, Powhatan had sent Newport twenty wild turkeys requesting twenty swords in exchange. Despite Smith's protests, Newport agreed to the trade. When Powhatan made a similar offer to Smith after Newport's departure, it was refused. There would be no further arms supplied to the natives if Smith had any say in the matter.

Undeterred, Powhatan instructed his braves to *take* what they could not obtain via trade and the colonists soon found themselves involved in a series of minor skirmishes with the local Indians. After one such attempt, Smith turned the tables, taking several Indians as his captives. Not long afterward, Pocahontas was sent by her father to negotiate the return of the prisoners. It is not known why Powhatan elected to send his young daughter rather than an older, perhaps more skillful, negotiator. However, some historians believe the crafty chief may have used Pocahontas to remind Smith of the debt he owed to her for his own life. Since she had saved his life months before, perhaps he would agree to spare the Indian captives. Whatever the reasons for Pocahontas coming to see Smith, the strategy worked.

After careful deliberations, Smith agreed to free the Indians—but only after they attended a church service at Jamestown. There is no historical evidence that explains Smith's insistence on the Indians' attendance at church and while no record of the participants exists, it is believed that Pocahontas may have also attended the service as a gesture of goodwill. Perhaps the Virginia Company's original directive to convert the natives to Christianity was the motivation for Smith's decision.

Explorations

Even though the coexistence between the colonists and the Indians was an uneasy one, John Smith felt the situation at Jamestown was calm enough for him to depart during the summer of 1608 on two more expeditions. Always mindful of the Virginia Company's directives with regard to finding gold and a route to the Pacific, John Smith and fourteen men set off in the shallop to explore and map the Chesapeake Bay and its primary rivers. Traveling some three thousand miles in an open boat, Smith found neither gold nor passage to the Pacific. He did, however, map, sketch, and name countless new rivers, streams, and landforms.

Returning from his journeys throughout the Chesapeake Bay region in September of 1608, Smith once again found trouble brewing at the Jamestown fort. Political turmoil involving its latest president, John Ratcliffe—who had been captain of the

A Painful Encounter

In addition to the plentiful wild game, Smith and his companions found the waters teeming with fish. In some cases the schools were so dense that the men could simply lower a sword into the water to catch dinner. Smith even wrote later that there was such an "abundance of fish lying so [thick] with their heads above water," that even without fishing nets, they "attempted to catch them with a frying pan."

One such marine encounter did not go well for Smith, though. Spearing an unusual-looking flattish fish with a long tail, Smith himself was skewered instead—by the poisonous barb of a stingray. Immediate and intense pain along with terrible swelling of Smith's shoulder, arm, and hand convinced him that death was soon to follow. Selecting a nearby spot for burial, Smith instructed his men to start digging. Fortunately, the application of a soothing salve by the physician traveling with the group brought relief. By evening, Smith felt well enough to eat the offending stingray for dinner. Stingray Point—at the mouth of the Rappahannock River—takes its name from Smith's painful encounter there.

Like a creature in flight, the stingray's graceful appearance seems at odds with its potential for injury. After his painful encounter with one, John Smith feared he was dying.

Discovery during the initial voyage to the New World—was resolved when Smith himself agreed to take over the job on September 10. Selected to serve a one-year term, Smith immediately got busy. Relations had cooled with the Powhatan Indians while Smith was away, and the colonists could not solely rely on them for food. If the Jamestown settlement was to survive another winter, the colonists had to get busy. In addition, when Christopher Newport returned from England that October with more supplies and settlers (including the first two women), those in Jamestown had no way of knowing that these would be the last supplies received from England for more than eighteen months.

Crowning Powhatan

During his most recent voyage to England, Newport was instructed by the Virginia Company to hold a ceremony in Jamestown crowning Powhatan as an emperor. In reality, the **coronation** ceremony was a trick to make Powhatan agree to become a subject of King James I. Knowing Powhatan would never fall for this, Smith strongly objected, but Newport was determined to carry out the orders from London. Invited to come to Jamestown for his crowning, Powhatan was no fool. Since he was already a king, Powhatan reasoned, what was the point of holding such a ceremony? He knew the English were planning some sort of trickery and insisted the ceremony be conducted at Werowocomoco.

The English complied with the request, but Newport and Smith arrived accompanied by 120 armed men. Smith, traveling by land, brought fifty of the men, and Newport came by water with the remaining seventy. Powhatan did not trust the Englishmen, and no doubt Pocahontas was also aware of her father's growing displeasure with the colonists. Despite elaborate gifts brought by the English—including a large canopy bed, various rings, a copper crown, and a bright red cloak—Powhatan was clearly irritated.

Refusing to kneel to be crowned, the great chief was eventually forced to his knees by Newport and two other Englishman. Once the crown was in place, a nearby soldier fired his pistol in the air—signaling Newport's barge to launch a volley of answering shots in salute. Misinterpreting the great noise from the ships, Powhatan leapt to his feet in alarm. Although he quickly regained his composure—and even offered some small gifts in return—Powhatan may have seen the mockery in this

Crowned in a mock ceremony at Werowocomoco, Powhatan was unimpressed by gifts from the English king.

so-called solemn royal ceremony as the final reason to break his already rapidly deteriorating relationship with the English.

Not long afterward, the chief told his people to stop trading with the colonists—probably not just because of the coronation event, but also because the summer of 1608 had been dry, and the resulting harvest was much poorer than usual. There simply wasn't enough food to spare.

Once again, conditions began to look grim at Jamestown. Despite her father's displeasure with the Englishmen, Pocahontas, it is believed, still came to the fort on occasion and may have even provided some much-needed food. Whether her father knew of her continued visits to the English is not known, but it seems few activities in his kingdom escaped Powhatan's notice. Taking her responsibilities toward her adopted brother, John Smith, very seriously was something that Pocahontas could not change just because her father was angry with the colonists. She owed obedience to Powhatan not only as his daughter, but also as his subject. Still, Pocahontas probably felt she owed something to the settlers she considered part of John Smith's family at Jamestown as well—especially after the role she may have played in Smith's rescue from death. This feeling of being caught between two worlds is something that would stay with Pocahontas for the rest of her life.

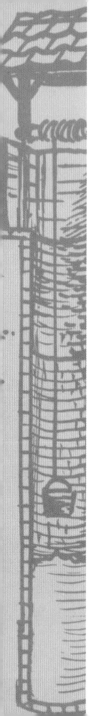

CHAPTER 8

Troubled Times

He that will not [work] shall not [eat].

—President John Smith to Jamestown colonists

In December of 1608, Christopher Newport sailed back to England. Included in the items he took back to London from Jamestown were John Smith's maps and drawings of the Chesapeake region as well as a no-holds-barred letter from Smith. The letter included his thoughts about what a disaster the idea of the coronation of Powhatan had been and his ongoing complaints about the laziness of the "gentlemen" settlers at Jamestown. Rather than welcome a thousand more of these lazy men, Smith's letter declared that he'd prefer to receive only "thirty Carpenters, [farmers], gardeners, fisher men, blacksmiths, masons, and diggers of trees."

Around Christmas, an unexpected summons came from Powhatan, asking to meet again at Werowocomoco reportedly to discuss trading for corn. Accompanied by forty-six well-armed, experienced soldiers and sailors, Smith fought the elements as he traveled by barge to Powhatan's encampment. Arriving in mid-January, Smith was greeted by the usual offerings of food and welcome. But Powhatan was quick to move to the real point of the meeting by asking bluntly when the Englishmen would be leaving the area for good. Despite the colony's weak start, Jamestown seemed to be holding its own. Powhatan was very aware of the growing number of settlers and supplies arriving and the colonists' increased trading and exploration in the area. Perhaps he was beginning to regret his earlier decision not to wipe out the fort when conditions there had been so poor.

Accompanied by forty-six well-armed, experienced soldiers and sailors, Smith . . . traveled by barge to Powhatan's encampment.

Although Smith did not know it yet, Powhatan had also already decided to abandon his encampment at Werowocomoco and move to a more remote location. (". . . my country," Powhatan would later tell Smith, "is large enough for me to go from you.") According to some historical accounts, while Smith was still in the midst of negotiations for corn, Powhatan made an excuse to leave his longhouse. Gathered outside were some of his warriors, his favorite wives, his children (including Pocahontas), and many of his belongings. Leaving several of his lesser wives behind to distract Smith and his party and keep them from growing suspicious, Powhatan departed.

Although warriors had been stationed to block the way out of the longhouse, Smith soon realized a trick had been played on him. He fired his pistol at those guarding the exit, and the Indians scattered. Smith then took the corn he needed at gunpoint. Returning with his party to their barge on the river, Smith found the vessel stranded by the low tide. Knowing the barge would not be free of the frozen muck until high tide came at around midnight, Smith and his men settled down uneasily to wait.

In the meantime, Powhatan, possibly hearing about the Englishmen's delay, sent a party of warriors back to the Werowocomoco site and sent word to Smith to join him again the next day for supper. The crafty chief tried to indicate that the entire incident had been a misunderstanding. Despite his suspicions that Powhatan was up to something, Smith made the decision to stay another day.

Warning in the Night

While traveling to Powhatan's new encampment with her family members, Pocahontas heard of her father's true plans. The offer of supper the next day actually concealed a plot to kill Smith and his men. Whether Pocahontas heard the news from someone else traveling in her group or directly from her father himself, the assumption was probably made by her companions that Pocahontas's loyalty to her own people would outweigh any thoughts of warning John Smith. That assumption proved to be incorrect.

Much later that evening, as Smith and his men were relaxing in anticipation of the next day's feast, they were startled by the appearance of Pocahontas. Having slipped away from her family, who were still traveling to the new encampment site, Pocahontas had walked quite some distance through the darkened woods to reach Smith. Her warning was simple. If they wanted to live, they should all leave quickly. She revealed that Powhatan was planning to feed the Englishmen the promised feast but would ask them to lay down their weapons while dining. As the unarmed men ate, the Indians would cut their throats.

Whether or not Pocahontas's earlier actions during Smith's rescue from being clubbed to death had been a true save or a carefully orchestrated ritual, this was clearly the real thing. Pocahontas had risked everything to save the Englishmen's lives. If anyone found out that Pocahontas had come to warn them, she, too, could face death. Setting aside her loyalty to her father and her tribe, Pocahontas had elected instead to warn Smith and his party of the plot to kill them.

Pocahontas appears part–Indian maiden, part–European lady in this undated engraving. As her friendship with John Smith deepened, the young woman probably began to feel pulled between two worlds.

Thinking how extremely brave her actions were, Smith probably wanted to give Pocahontas some sort of present to thank her for her efforts, and he brought out several blue glass beads. Seeing the trinkets in Smith's hand, Pocahontas reacted—according to reports by others in the party—with tears streaming. Didn't Smith realize that, if she took the beads, Pocahontas would have to explain how she got them? Didn't he also realize just how great the chance was that she took in coming to warn him of the plot? Did he really value their friendship so little that he would simply pay her with a few beads as he would any local guide?

No factual evidence exists as to whether the relationship between John Smith and Pocahontas was something deeper than an adopted brother-sister bond. However, all do agree that theirs was—at the very least—a strong friendship. But after a final glance at Smith, Pocahontas ran out into the night. Their friendship—which now seemed of so little value to Smith—had apparently ended.

Their friendship—which now seemed of so little value to Smith—had apparently ended.

Not long afterward, the promised feast was presented to Smith and his men, and platters heaped with turkey, beans, squash, and venison were served. Keeping Pocahontas's warning foremost in his mind, Smith insisted that the food be taste-tested by the Indians as an added precaution before he and his men would eat. When Powhatan's warriors suggested that the colonists might be more comfortable if they removed their weapons, Smith disregarded it. He and his men kept their weapons at the ready by their sides throughout the meal.

No attacks took place, and, after a very wakeful night, Smith's party sailed safely out on the next morning's rising tide. Once again, John Smith owed Pocahontas his life, but the Powhatan princess would never visit her adopted brother in Jamestown again.

Taking Strong Action

After Smith and his men returned from their near-death experience at Werowocomoco in January of 1609, Indian attacks on Jamestown increased. As usual, Smith found that little worthwhile work had been done at the fort in his absence. The limited stores of food were overrun with rats and worms. Tools and some weapons had disappeared—likely stolen by local Indians. Fortunately, with the food Smith had brought from Werowocomoco, the colonists would be able to survive the worst of the winter months.

Smith now thought it was time for a stronger course of action, and he gathered the colonists together. Tired of what appeared to be habitual laziness among the "gentlemen" colonists, he laid down the law. If the colonists wanted food, they would have to work for it. In his position as president, Smith coolly reminded the group that he was in charge. Although some grumbled about Smith's hard line, his threats seemed to work. During the next three months, twenty houses were

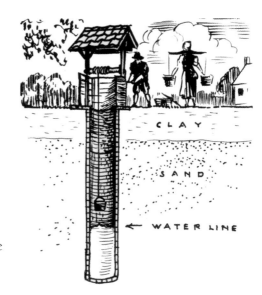

During John Smith's presidency, a brick-lined well was constructed to provide much-needed fresh water to the Jamestown colonists.

CLAY

SAND

← WATER LINE

constructed, and a well was dug that brought fresh, clean water to the thirsty colonists. Some thirty to forty acres of crops were planted, and guards were posted at the neck of the peninsula to warn of invaders.

Having noted the Indians' successful methods of living off the land, Smith tried to mirror the Indians' example. By spring, he had organized the colonists into small, self-sustaining twenty- or thirty-man groups for survival. One group was sent to the mouth of the bay to fish; another was dispatched downriver to live off the plentiful oysters there. Another group was sent to stay with friendly Indians nearby. Individual interactions between settlers and natives benefited both sides. The English learned proven techniques for living off the land from the natives, while the Indians advanced their limited technological skills—especially in the use of firearms and tools. Although some settlers grumbled about the arrangements, no one starved. Jamestown was surviving.

But John Smith's stern orders and harsh ways made him increasingly unpopular with the colonists—especially those "gentlemen" who so disliked work of any kind. Despite the fact that the colony seemed at last to be productive, many Jamestown residents were pleased by the news that arrived that summer. Captain Samuel Argall sailed in from England with word that a fleet of ships would soon be arriving. Onboard were six hundred new settlers, plenty of supplies, and—most importantly—news of a reorganization of the Virginia Company and a revised charter for the Jamestown colony. The office of president was no more. Instead, there would be a new governor. John Smith, it appeared, was out of a job.

Out of Office

Furious that he had been simply cast aside—despite all his hard work—Smith refused to give up his role as president until his present term was up or the new governor arrived in Jamestown, whichever came first. Gradually, ships began to arrive at Jamestown—the *Blessing,* the *Lion*, the *Falcon*, the *Unity*, the *Swallow*, and the *Diamond*. Battered and bruised, with torn sails, broken masts, and many ill or injured passengers, all the ships had encountered severe storms and many other difficulties. But there was still no sign of the *Sea Venture*, the **flagship** on which Sir Thomas Gates, the deputy governor, and other new council members had been sailing. Many in the colony began to wonder if the ship and all onboard had been lost at sea. Unbeknownst to all, the *Sea Venture* had been caught by storms and had run aground in Bermuda. It would be a long time before those traveling on the ship would be heard from.

Finally, with little time remaining in his term, it is believed that Smith turned in his resignation to the remaining council members. Fed up with the political infighting that now seemed to consume the Jamestown populace, Smith and a group of men from the fort traveled upriver in late August in the hopes of

The *Sea Venture*

The doomed flagship of the Virginia Company—the three-hundred-ton *Sea Venture*—was part of a convoy of vessels sailing from England to Jamestown in the summer of 1609. Onboard were three high-ranking officials headed for the new colony—Sir Thomas Gates, deputy governor; Sir George Somers, admiral of the fleet; and Vice Admiral Christopher Newport, captain of the *Sea Venture*. While en route that July, the *Sea Venture* ran aground on a Bermuda reef during a severe hurricane. Fortunately, all 150 people onboard survived and were able to make it onto the then-uninhabited island. For nine months they lived off fish, sea turtles, and wild hogs. Using materials salvaged from the *Sea Venture*, as well as local Bermuda cypress wood, the survivors eventually constructed two smaller ships—the *Deliverance* and the *Patience*. They were then able to complete their voyage to Virginia some six hundred miles to the northwest, and they arrived at their destination in May of 1610. The story of the *Sea Venture* and its wreck are believed by some scholars to have served as the inspiration for William Shakespeare's final play, *The Tempest*.

Storm-tossed and feared lost by those in Jamestown, settlers aboard the *Sea Venture* were marooned in Bermuda for nine months.

resuming some sort of trading system with the Powhatan Indians. Smith may have also hoped to find a peaceful location in which he himself could settle, removed from the constant arguing and upheaval in Jamestown. Regardless, he was unsuccessful on all counts. Nine months after Pocahontas had warned Smith and his party of the dinnertime attempt on their lives, the Indians were still annoyed with Smith and his fellow Englishmen. No welcome was offered. Reluctantly, Smith decided to return to Jamestown.

On the journey back to Jamestown, tragedy struck. It is believed that Smith was resting in the bottom of his boat—weapon at

. . . the Indians were still annoyed with Smith and his fellow Englishmen.

his side and bag of gunpowder tied firmly to his waist—when a spark or cinder fell onto the bag causing it to explode. Writing later of what had happened (in the third person, as before), Smith's description is horrifying: The freak accident "tore the flesh from his body and thighs, nine or ten inches square, in the most frightful manner. To quench the tormenting fire, frying him in his clothes, he leaped [overboard] into the deep river, where, ere they could recover him, he was nearly drowned." Narrowly escaping death, Smith—with the help of his men—was able to make it back to Jamestown. Knowing his recovery would be a lengthy one, Smith opted to return to England. Flat on his back, he knew he had little chance of challenging those now holding authority at the fort. Sailing on October 1, 1609, John Smith left Virginia behind forever.

Some historians believe that not long after Smith set sail for England, Pocahontas returned to the Jamestown fort. Whether she had heard of her friend's injuries and wanted to be sure he was

Arm raised in a gesture of friendship, Pocahontas travels to visit the Jamestown colonists in this early 19th-century engraving.

healing, or she had no knowledge about his terrible accident at all, Pocahontas was entirely unprepared for the news of Smith's departure. Although some at the settlement knew who the young woman was, they did not welcome her. To those newly arrived from England, she was simply another Indian. Any attempts to reestablish friendly relations with Powhatan and his nation had ended with the departure of John Smith. Her English friend was gone, and likely dead, they told Pocahontas. They told her she should leave. There was nothing for her at the fort anymore. Stepping back into the woodlands, Pocahontas turned her back on the people of Jamestown.

CHAPTER 9

On Her Own

Pocahontas lay concealed, thinking herself safe, and unknown to all but trusty Friends.

—William Stith, colonist and historian

After being told of John Smith's death and walking out of the Jamestown settlement, Pocahontas had no contact with the colonists for several years. Not much is known about events in her life during this period. Regardless, it is safe to assume that Pocahontas felt tremendous grief over the likelihood of Smith's death. No matter what their relationship—adopted siblings, friends, or something more—he had been an enormously important presence in her life, and his loss must have been heart-wrenching for the young woman.

By 1610, according to the custom of her tribe, Pocahontas—now perhaps fifteen—was old enough to marry, and many historians think that she did. It is believed she married an Indian warrior named Kocoum who may have been from the Patawomeck tribe. Writings of the time indicate that an Indian bride usually was ceremonially purchased during the marriage ritual. A string of beads was broken over the couple's joined hands and the fallen beads were given in payment to the bride's father. The ending of a marriage was equally uncomplicated: Husband and wife simply said the words "I divorce you" three times and the union was over. Since no husband was in evidence in 1613 when Pocahontas next came in contact with the English, it is assumed that her marriage had ended—either by mutual agreement or because of Kocoum's death.

Life among the Patawomeck

Regardless of how long Pocahontas's first marriage lasted, in the spring of 1613, she was a single woman living about one hundred miles to the north of Jamestown among the Patawomeck people. It is not certain how long Pocahontas had been with the Patawomeck, but one theory is that she had come for a visit of several months in order to represent her father in regional trade negotiations among area tribes. Others think she may have selected the area as a refuge of some sort and lived there for a long period of time. The eighteenth century historian William Stith, who wrote about this phase in Pocahontas's life, suggests that she may have left her father's lands to get away from all the fighting between her people and the English, whose thoughtless actions had led to more bloodshed. It was now out of her hands—especially with the departure of Smith.

. . . it is safe to assume that Pocahontas felt tremendous grief over the likelihood of Smith's death.

Pocahontas also might have felt safer farther from Powhatan's reach. Although once her father's favorite, by now the young woman had defied the great chief on more than one occasion and may have been unsure of her reception at home. She also experienced a series of difficult events. She was separated from her mother at an early age. She was affected by the strained relations she had experienced between her own people and the newly arrived English. She felt great sorrow over the reported death of

Little is known of Pocahontas's life during the four-year period after John Smith left Jamestown for good. Maturing into womanhood, she had no contact with the English colonists.

John Smith. Finally, she lost her husband through death or divorce. These events may have changed the lively and playful child into a more withdrawn and private young woman. Few outside the Patawomeck people reportedly knew that Pocahontas was staying in the area.

In the four years since Pocahontas had turned her back on the Jamestown fort, the colonists had suffered badly. Named the "Starving Time" by John Smith in his later writings, the winter of 1609–1610 was the worst endured thus far. Of the five or six hundred people who had settled at the fort when John Smith sailed for England that October, nearly 90 percent had died by the following May when the *Deliverance* and the *Patience* sailed up the James River. Onboard were the survivors from the *Sea Venture*, which had been wrecked in Bermuda. Arriving onshore and seeing the dire conditions, Sir Thomas Gates immediately rang the church bell to call the colonists together. Stranded in Bermuda by fierce storms, the former passengers of the *Sea Venture* had sailed into Jamestown with barely enough food onboard for a few days. Expecting a thriving settlement with plenty of supplies, the newly arrived settlers found that those at Jamestown were in serious trouble. Even the Indians were short on food due to poor harvests. After two weeks, Gates made the difficult decision to abandon the fort. All remaining colonists would return to England. As Indian lookouts watched the pathetic band depart and sail away, they could scarcely wait to deliver the news to Powhatan. At last, the English were leaving—or so it seemed.

> *. . . the newly arrived settlers found that those at Jamestown were in serious trouble.*

Ironically, as the *Deliverance* and the *Patience* made their way down the James River at dawn on June 8, 1610, a longboat was spied traveling upriver. Those onboard were from the British flagship *De La Warre*, and they were headed to Jamestown. The *De La Warre* carried 150 settlers, enough food and supplies for a year, and Lord De La Warre, who would head the colonial government. Taking these events as a sign from God, the *Deliverance* and the *Patience* turned around and headed back to the fort. Jamestown was reborn.

Lord De La Warre, continually plagued by illness since his arrival in Virginia, was replaced the following spring by Sir Thomas Dale. Dale was a stern taskmaster who treated misbehaving colonists and local tribesmen with equal brutality. Indian attacks took place on a fairly regular basis and netted captives on both sides. The Powhatan people had also captured

The Starving Time

Studying clues left behind, archaeologists have confirmed that the winter of 1609–1610 was probably the worst Jamestown colonists experienced. With stored corn long gone, the English resorted to eating whatever they could find—mice, rats, dogs, cats, and even poisonous snakes. Boiling shirts and cuffs produced edible starch that was made into a kind of porridge, and even belts, book covers, and leather door hinges were cooked and consumed. Reports of cannibalism remain unconfirmed. But some without hope reportedly did dig their own graves, climb in, and wait for death.

While in the past, much of blame for this period of starvation had been placed on the idleness of many of the Jamestown settlers, scientists today believe that a severe area-wide drought may have also been a factor. Unfortunately for the English, their arrival in Virginia coincided with the height of a seven-year dry spell—the worst seen in that area in nearly eight centuries. By studying the rings of cypress trees in the area, scientists can see that their growth was seriously stunted by the drought. Regardless of the cause of the Starving Time, it was yet another example that life in the new colony wasn't easy. Scientists today estimate that less than one-fourth of the roughly six thousand people who arrived on Virginia shores between the years of 1607 and 1624 survived.

Rations dwindled to almost nothing during the winter of 1609–1610. Referred to as the Starving Time by Smith and later historians, Jamestown's population was nearly wiped out.

Ready to abandon the Jamestown fort in 1610, departing colonists were halted by the arrival of English ships bearing much-needed supplies and scores of new settlers.

or stolen English weapons. Despite the hostile climate, however, Jamestown seemed to prosper. By the early months of 1613, as Pocahontas was living with the Patawomeck people some distance away, more than seven hundred colonists—among them at least thirty women—had settled in Virginia.

Kidnapped!

Also visiting the lands of the Patawomeck in 1613 was the privateer Samuel Argall, who was on a trading mission for the Jamestown colony. (Argall was the same Englishmen who—in the summer of 1609—had brought news of the pending arrival of a new governor and the ousting of John Smith as president of the colony.) Reportedly, Argall learned of Pocahontas's presence in the area by accident. But he quickly realized her potential as a hostage in negotiations with Powhatan. If Argall could kidnap the chief's favorite daughter, Powhatan would have no choice but to agree to a peaceful settlement with the English. Argall was wise enough to realize that trying to take Pocahontas by force was out of the question. He had to find some way to trick her into returning to Jamestown under his guard.

Reportedly, Argall learned of Pocahontas's presence in the area quite by accident.

Opportunity soon presented itself in the form of Japazaws, a low-ranking Patawomeck chief. An acquaintance of Argall's, the chief was always interested in acquiring English goods—particularly copper. When told of the plan to kidnap Pocahontas, Japazaws hesitated at first. If he did not help, threatened Argall, it would mean the end of both their friendship and their trading relationship. But, argued Japazaws, if he did help, his involvement might bring war with the great chief Powhatan. If it came to war, reasoned Argall, the English would aid the Patawomeck. Well aware of the increasing numbers of English settlers moving into the lands along the Chesapeake, Japazaws saw their potential for taking over the area. He agreed to help Samuel Argall kidnap Pocahontas.

Accurately sensing that Pocahontas would not easily be tricked, Japazaws enlisted his wife's help to get the young woman to come to the waterfront. No record exists of how Pocahontas arrived there—perhaps an afternoon walk had been suggested, or an errand along the shoreline. No matter the deception, Pocahontas found herself near the water's edge. Then the questions began: Had Pocahontas heard that there was an English ship—the *Treasurer*—at anchor? Would she like to go see it? Perhaps it was her memories of John Smith—or simply curiosity—but Pocahontas agreed.

Once there, Japazaws and his wife engaged in an elaborate bit of play-acting. Pleading with her husband to take her onboard to

Samuel Argall (c. 1572–c. 1626)

Arguably one of the Virginia Company's less-admirable employees, Samuel Argall was commissioned admiral of Virginia in 1610. Given the task of finding a shorter route between England and its new colony, Argall is most famous for his capture of Pocahontas in April of 1613. Named deputy governor of Virginia in 1616, Argall stepped into the top slot for three years in the absence of the colony's then-governor. Known for his harsh and unpopular rule, Argall next went on to captain a twenty-four-gun merchant ship in 1620. Two years later, he became a member of the council for New England and received a knighthood. In 1625, as a member of the British king's war council, Argall was put in command of a twenty-eight-ship fleet that fought—unsuccessfully—against the Spanish in Cádiz. Never married, Argall is believed to have died at sea in 1626.

Samuel Argall, captor of Pocahontas, is depicted here greeting members of Virginia's Chickahominy tribe.

see the ship up close, Japazaws's wife was firmly turned down by her husband. It was not acceptable. She could not go on such an excursion alone. She would not be allowed onboard without another woman as her escort. Although Japazaws's wife begged and cried, her husband stood firm. She simply could not venture onto the ship without another female accompanying her. Both looked at Pocahontas. Would she be willing to go aboard the ship as the companion of Japazaws's wife?

Accurately sensing that Pocahontas would not easily be tricked, Japazaws enlisted his wife's help . . .

At some point, Argall himself smoothly stepped forward with an invitation for the three of them to dine onboard with him—thereby increasing the appeal of the short excursion. Still Pocahontas hesitated. Knowing of her people's mistrust of the English and their ships—where one might be shot or thrown overboard or worse—she did not want to go. But, at last, the wailing and pleading of Japazaws's wife became too much. Pocahontas agreed to go onboard the *Treasurer* and dine with the captain and her friends. The trap was set.

After the meal, English custom dictated that a rest was in order, and Pocahontas was taken to the gunner's room (the area where weapons were typically stored) to nap. But the young woman grew increasingly uneasy and could not rest. Something was wrong—what, she wasn't certain—but she knew it was time to join her friends, get off the ship, and return to shore. But, unbeknownst to Pocahontas, in the time since lunch had ended, Japazaws and his wife had already returned to shore— now in possession of a shiny copper kettle that was their payment for helping the English. With her exit barred, Pocahontas found herself held captive on the English ship by Captain Samuel Argall and his crew of sixty men.

CHAPTER 10

A Changed Life

. . . for the good of the plantation, the honor of our country, for the glory of God, for mine own salvation. . . .

—John Rolfe, on his reasons for wanting to
marry Pocahontas

Once his prize was safely onboard, Samuel Argall no doubt congratulated himself on the successful capture of Pocahontas. Before setting sail for Jamestown, he sent a native tribesman—possibly a Patawomeck guide—with a message informing Powhatan "that I had taken his daughter, and if he would send home the Englishmen whom he detained in slavery, with such arms and tools as the Indians had gotten and [stolen], and also a great quantity of corn, that then he should have his daughter restored, otherwise not."

Accounts differ as to Pocahontas's reaction when informed by Argall that she was being taken back to Jamestown to be exchanged for English prisoners and arms. Some reports note that she was "despondent and pensive" on the voyage but seemed resigned to her fate by the time the *Treasurer* dropped anchor at Jamestown.

Arriving at the settlement, Argall turned the negotiations—and his prisoner—over to Sir Thomas Gates, now the colonial governor. Assuming Powhatan would comply very quickly with the terms for his daughter's

Tricked into boarding the English ship the *Treasurer*, Pocahontas was betrayed by Japazaws, a low-ranking Patawomeck chief. In this 1910 painting, Captain Argall delivers his captive to Jamestown.

release, Gates was surprised when the chief called the captors' bluff. Requesting that his daughter not be mistreated, Powhatan freed the English captives and sent a canoe full of corn to Jamestown—but no weapons were returned and no further word was heard.

Powhatan had no intention of making peace with the English—regardless of how much sadness the loss of his daughter must have caused him. In actuality, Powhatan had little to fear with regard to his daughter's safety. Pocahontas, being the daughter of what amounted to Tidewater royalty, had become something of a celebrity among the colonists. Governor Gates treated the captive with respect and others followed his lead. The chief's daughter, noted one writer of the time, was "very well and [kindly treated]."

Weaponry

Contrary to what Powhatan may have believed, his warriors definitely had firepower superior to that of the newly arrived English settlers. While it was possible for a bow and arrow to be fired six times in a single minute, it could take as long as thirty seconds for a colonist to shoot his gun just once. Chosen because it was inexpensive, tough, and relatively easy to repair, the matchlock musket was the primary weapon used by the early Jamestown settlers. Unfortunately, these guns were also heavy (about sixteen pounds) and awkward to fire. A skilled Indian hunter might hit a moving target some forty yards away, but English muskets were nearly worthless beyond a distance of ten yards. One factor the colonists did have in their favor, though, was the thundering, earsplitting, frightening noise produced when a musket was fired. It was a sound that most Powhatan warriors had never heard before—and it scared them.

With matchlock musket at the ready and sword by his side, this Jamestown sentry is well armed.

Christian Convert

Not having visited Jamestown in at least three years, Pocahontas probably found much changed. Few, if any, of the original colonists remained from the carefree, cartwheeling visits of her childhood. The fort itself had grown into a town and now stretched across the peninsula and onto the mainland. The church had been enlarged and expanded, and many new homes and other structures had been built. Jamestown itself had begun to resemble an English village—with gardens and a market square. Few trappings of its original rough-and-ready appearance remained.

Eventually realizing that Powhatan probably had no intention of ransoming his daughter, Sir Thomas Dale, the colony's marshal, instead decided on a plan to convert the Indian princess to Christianity. After all, religious conversion of the natives had been one of the original directives of the Virginia Company, and what better example could there be than the daughter of a famous chief?

. . . Sir Thomas Dale, the colony's marshal, instead decided on a plan to convert the Indian princess to Christianity.

Reverend Alexander Whitaker, who resided upriver from Jamestown at Henrico—the colony's second settlement, established by Dale—was elected to instruct Pocahontas in her new faith. The fact that Whitaker's hundred-acre **parsonage** was surrounded by five forts was also an important consideration. Here, Pocahontas would be under close guard should any tribesmen attempt to recapture her.

In addition to her religious conversion, Pocahontas was also expected to learn—and adopt—the ways of the British. Therefore, she received daily instruction in areas such as manners, dress, speech, and the various qualities of an English Christian lady.

By all accounts, Pocahontas was a quick study. Perhaps it was the years spent by herself apart from her father's people. Perhaps it was the gentleness and kindness with which she was treated. Perhaps she felt abandoned by her father. For whatever reason, Pocahontas responded positively to her instruction in English ways. Her curiosity and intelligence were apparent to all as she memorized the prayers of the Church of England and began to speak this new language. One eighteenth-century historian wrote that Pocahontas "expressed an eager desire, and [showed] great capacity in learning." After studying the English ways for some time, Pocahontas appeared to openly reject her Indian culture.

No longer dressed in the deerskin skirt of her tribesmen, Pocahontas was instead laced into a snug-fitting corset, her arms covered by long sleeves and her legs by an ankle-length gown. Hard-soled shoes replaced her soft moccasins. The Indian princess had been transformed into a proper English gentlewoman, and her quiet beauty soon caught the eye of another Henrico churchgoer.

Giving up her Native American past and accepting Christianity meant adopting English dress and customs. This engraving may have been based on a portrait of Pocahontas painted during her lifetime.

Marriage

John Rolfe was then a twenty-eight-year-old widower who had lost both his wife and infant daughter just a few years before. Since arriving in Jamestown, he had experienced increasing success as a tobacco farmer, especially after experimenting with new strains that were milder than the native plants grown by the Indians. Rolfe and Pocahontas probably first met in church. Soon they began to spend time together—carefully chaperoned—at the parsonage. Helping Pocahontas with her prayers and studies, Rolfe realized his feelings were deepening. Although no record exists, many believe that Pocahontas returned his affections. After the events of Pocahontas's life, Rolfe may have represented a sense of calm and stability she had not experienced. But Rolfe, born in England and raised a Christian, was uncertain if his feelings for Pocahontas were appropriate. After all, she was considered a savage by his fellow countrymen. Even though she was learning the English language and customs, she was still considered a heathen because her actual conversion to Christianity had not yet taken place.

Soon they began to spend time together—carefully chaperoned—at the parsonage.

When John Rolfe's thoughts turned to marriage, he knew it was time to act. Fearful of the reaction of his friend and the colony's acting governor, Sir Thomas Dale, Rolfe wrote a letter presenting the idea as a business proposition and asked for permission to marry Pocahontas. Although the lengthy letter mainly sounds like an official document, at one point Rolfe cannot help himself. "It is Pocahontas, to whom my hearty and best thoughts are, and have been a long time so entangled, and enthralled in so intricate a labyrinth."

John Rolfe and Tobacco

Jamestown colonists, accustomed to the milder tobacco favored by Europeans, cared little for the harsher-flavored tobacco plants grown by Native Americans. Knowing the smoking preferences of his fellow Englishmen, John Rolfe began successful experimental plantings of a new strain of tobacco in 1612. One of the *Sea Venture* survivors, Rolfe is believed to have obtained tobacco seeds during his time in the West Indies. Sweeter and more fragrant, this new variety grew well in the Virginia soil. After Rolfe's friends pronounced his tobacco "pleasant, [sweet], and strong," a large enough quantity was eventually harvested to send a sample shipment to England, where it was well received. By 1620, the Jamestown colony exported some fifty thousand pounds of the new strain. Over the years, Rolfe continued his efforts to improve the new Virginia tobacco, and he is credited with helping to develop a strong economic base in the English colony.

Tobacco eventually became a major crop for the Jamestown colonists who are depicted harvesting the fragrant leaves in this modern-day painting.

To Dale, this seemed like an excellent idea. With the joining of the two cultures, perhaps peace with the Powhatan people might be attained at last. But first, Dale decided to make one final attempt to recapture the stolen English weapons. In March 1614, Dale, Rolfe, and Pocahontas, accompanied by 150 armed men, journeyed to visit Powhatan. Two of her half brothers came to see their sister and reported back to their father that—despite her somewhat unusual attire—she appeared to be in good health. They were told by Pocahontas that the English were treating her well and she had made her future plans.

She expressed to her half brothers that if her father truly loved her, he would have gladly returned the stolen English weapons. Obviously, they were more valuable to Powhatan than she was. Therefore, she had made the decision to stay with the English who did love and value her. When no response came from Powhatan, the party returned to Henrico. There is no record of Pocahontas's reaction to what appeared to be her father's final rejection.

In this c. 1655 print, Pocahontas (circled) is visiting with her half brothers. During this visit, Pocahontas was wearing English-style clothing, which surprised the half brothers. This print is not accurate, however, and shows her in traditional dress.

Eventually, however, word reached Powhatan that John Rolfe wished to marry his daughter. Now about eighty years old, Powhatan was tired of fighting with the English. Surprising Thomas Dale, the old chief spoke of peace and even offered to return some of the missing weapons. Although he would not attend the wedding, he would send one of his brothers to represent him. Among his gifts to Pocahontas were a string of freshwater pearls and several parcels of land. Prior to the marriage, which took place on April 5, 1614, Pocahontas was baptized in the Church of England—thereby renouncing her Native American spiritual heritage and accepting the Christian faith as her own. Taking the name Rebecca, she began her new life.

One of eight huge oil paintings displayed in the U.S. Capitol rotunda, this famous 19th-century work depicts the baptism of Pocahontas just prior to her marriage to John Rolfe.

CHAPTER 11

Rebecca Rolfe

At last rejecting her barbarous condition, she was married to an English Gentleman.

—*John Smith, in a letter to Queen Anne*

With the 1614 marriage of Pocahontas to John Rolfe, an eight-year period began that colonial historians refer to as the Peace of Pocahontas. Tired of continually warring with the English, Chief Powhatan agreed to lay down his arms and coexist with the colonists whose numbers were rapidly swelling. (Within twenty years of John Smith's 1607 arrival some fifteen thousand settlers would eventually stream onto Virginia shores.) The tide had turned, and Powhatan knew he could not stem the flood. Others might try—and did—but his days of mighty battles were over.

The wedding of Pocahontas and John Rolfe is believed to have been the first recorded marriage between a Native American and a European.

No written record exists detailing the first months of the Rolfes' marriage, but one can probably assume that they began to settle into the little routines of daily life—establishing their home, planning their future. John Rolfe may have viewed his new wife's working knowledge of Native American tobacco-growing practices as an added asset in their partnership. While Powhatan men were the ones to grow and cultivate tobacco, Pocahontas's keen powers of observation had helped her pick up a great deal of practical information, which Rolfe applied to his own crops. Fish, for example, worked well as a fertilizer for the growing crops, and the young plants seemed to thrive when planted with a southern exposure.

Early in the year following her marriage, Pocahontas—now known to the English as Rebecca Rolfe—gave birth to a son. The Rolfes named the baby Thomas in honor of their friend and **benefactor**, Sir Thomas Dale. The baby was born at Varina, the Rolfes' home located near Henrico. (*Varina* was the name of a mild variety of Spanish tobacco that was similar to the new type of plant that John Rolfe was growing.) The land upon which Varina was built is believed

Not long after her marriage to John Rolfe, Pocahontas gave birth to her only child—a son named after the family's friend and benefactor, Sir Thomas Dale.

to have been a wedding gift from Powhatan to his daughter. "She lives civilly and lovingly with him," wrote Thomas Dale of Pocahontas's relationship with her husband.

A Visit to London

While still serving as Virginia's governor, Dale became concerned about Londoners' recent lack of interest in the Jamestown colony. Londoners now seemed more curious about a new settlement that was being established on the island of Bermuda. Fearful that a loss of interest would lead to a loss of revenue, Dale began to think of ways to rekindle interest in Jamestown.

Planning to travel to London the following spring, he invited the Rolfe family to join him. Not only would Pocahontas have a chance to see England in all its aristocratic glory, England would have the opportunity to meet a real Native American princess. What better way could there be, Dale theorized, to renew Londoners' fascination with the Virginia colony? The Virginia Company agreed with Dale and offered an annual income to Pocahontas in appreciation of her willingness to travel overseas on their behalf.

For John Rolfe, now Secretary of the Virginia Colony, the trip would offer him a chance to promote the Jamestown colony as a wise business opportunity. He hoped to encourage people in London to invest in the colony. As befitting a true princess, Pocahontas planned to make the journey accompanied by an **entourage** consisting of about a dozen or so Native Americans. Among them was her sister Matachanna, who was there to help take care of the Rolfes' baby son.

Pocahontas was already familiar with the ship that would carry her family across the Atlantic in 1616. Aboard the 130-ton *Treasurer*, Pocahontas had literally been transported from one life to another as Samuel Argall's captive in 1613. Compared to the simple dugout canoes of the Powhatan people, this vessel with its many masts and square-rigged sails was an impressive sight—at least when viewed from the Virginia shoreline. But once the ship was tossed about by the Atlantic's massive waves, the small and cramped accommodations for the hundred or so aboard became increasingly oppressive.

While her husband had already made one such crossing, Pocahontas was unprepared for the experience. Facilities, such as they were, were extremely primitive. Rats, roaches, and other **vermin** roamed freely. After the few buckets of water brought onboard at the journey's start were drained, one could only hope for a rainstorm to refill them. Sailing eastward aboard the *Treasurer*, John Rolfe probably prayed that a fate similar to that of the *Sea Venture* did not await his family. Many weeks after their departure from Virginia, everyone in the group was relieved to see the English coastline finally come into sight in early June.

London, as viewed by Pocahontas, was a place of many people, much noise, and constant activity. The charming young woman won the city's respect.

After a week-long trip of some 180 miles cross-country by coach, Pocahontas finally caught sight of London for the first time. Accustomed to the peace and beauty of the Eastern Woodlands, she was probably stunned by the seemingly endless chimneys, rooftops, carriages, smoke, sound, and *people*. People were everywhere. *No wonder the English wanted to colonize the New World*, Pocahontas may have thought. *They have run out of room in their own country.* One of the Indians traveling with Pocahontas would later tell Powhatan that there were as many English "as the stars in the sky, the sand on the English beaches, or the leaves on the trees."

Soon after arriving in London and settling in the accommodations the Virginia Company had rented for the Rolfe family's stay, Pocahontas was befriended by Lady De La Warre. The statesman's wife made sure the younger women had the proper clothes and other attire, and arranged for Pocahontas's introduction to various members of the English aristocracy as well as other public figures such as the bishop of London.

At first, the Indian princess was viewed as a curiosity, but soon she was appreciated for her charm, her grace, and her intelligence. Although often addressed by her English name, Rebecca Rolfe, the young woman was quickly recognized as the daughter of a king and treated as such by those that met her. Accompanied by her husband and others in her party, she was wined and dined at various parties and events throughout her time in London.

At first, the Indian princess was viewed as a curiosity, but soon she was appreciated for her charm, her grace, and her intelligence.

Presented to King James I along with her husband, John Rolfe, the Powhatan princess bows to English royalty.

Waiting for John Smith

During these exciting times, Pocahontas received some shocking news—John Smith was alive and well. He was not only alive; he was staying right there in London. Smith had been on an expedition to the New England region, but had recently returned. Eagerly awaiting his visit—for he was certain to know of her arrival and even more certain to want to see her—Pocahontas was soon disappointed. John Smith did not come.

Surely, she would see him at one of the many social events and other functions the Virginia Company had arranged for her to attend, but he was not at any. Eventually, Pocahontas's disappointment turned to hurt and then to anger. She could not understand why he was ignoring her. But Pocahontas had no way of knowing that John Smith had indeed been thinking of her—so much so that he had written a lengthy letter to Queen Anne about

Learning during her London visit that John Smith (shown at right) was alive was surprising news to Pocahontas, but her old friend's apparent reluctance to visit made her disappointed and angry.

what a fine person Pocahontas was and how much the Jamestown settlers owed her.

At the Twelfth Night revels—held on the last night of the Christmas celebration—the royal family sponsored a series of feasts and performances. To be invited was considered a great honor. When the princess of the Virginia woodlands met with the English queen, it was truly a meeting of equals, as they both stood as personal representatives of their people and their people's accomplishments.

Many more weeks passed—still with no word or visit from John Smith. The dampness and cold of the English air began to affect the Indians, and two eventually died. After a while, Pocahontas and her companions moved out of London to the town of Brentford. It was hoped that the clearer air of the English countryside might improve the Indians' health. By that point, even Pocahontas had developed a cough that settled in her chest. (Some later historians believe this may have been the beginning stages of tuberculosis.) It was here in Brentford, where she was hoping to restore her strength, that Pocahontas at last encountered John Smith.

Eight long years had passed since the two had spoken—and their last parting had not been a happy one. Risking her own life

Leaving the smoky congestion of London behind, Pocahontas and her party sought solitude in the English countryside near Brentford (depicted above).

in an attempt to save her friend's, Pocahontas's efforts had been barely acknowledged by John Smith, who seemed to treat her as he would a guide. Smith had now had more than enough time to reflect upon his actions and, if he did so, he may have felt embarrassed by how clumsy and ungracious his earlier behavior appeared. He may also have felt uncomfortable about his own lack of importance or sense of accomplishment.

Whereas Pocahontas and her family were now the toast of London, he was only a simple soldier with little of the status he once held in Jamestown. Regardless of the events past or the present, though, John Smith knew he could not delay his visit to Pocahontas any longer.

John Smith's Explorations

At the time that John Smith met Pocahontas in England, he might have felt somewhat insignificant compared to her prominence. But history has shown his contribution to the settlement and exploration of America to be invaluable. In 2007, to celebrate his efforts, a team of modern-day explorers retraced much of the summer journey John Smith made some four centuries before. Unlike Smith's all-male crew, which included a carpenter, blacksmith, physician, and several soldiers, the 2007 team of seven men and five women was largely composed of naturalists, historians, and educators.

Although no detailed records describing Smith's original vessel exist, the twenty-eight-foot replica built for the 2007 voyage is thought to be similar in design. Constructed using many seventeenth-century shipbuilding tools and methods, the modern-day shallop had one mast, one sail, and eight sixteen-foot, twenty-five-pound oars. Like Smith's ship, it offered little in the way of protection from the elements.

Over the course of more than four months, the twelve crew-members rowed and sailed to more than two dozen ports between Jamestown, Virginia, and Port Deposit, Maryland, highlighting many of Smith's original routes of exploration.

Photographed during the 2007 re-creation of John Smith's Chesapeake Bay travels, this modern-day shallop carried a dozen crew members to more than two dozen ports.

CHAPTER 12

Death on English Soil

. . . I will be forever and ever your countryman.
—Pocahontas to John Smith, 1617

John Smith's visit to Pocahontas is believed to have occurred in either January or February of 1617. All agree that she had no advance knowledge of the event. One day Smith was just *there* in the doorway of the Brentford country house. In fact, his appearance was so startling to Pocahontas that she was simply unable to speak. "Without any words," wrote Smith later, "she turned about, obscured her face, as not seeming well contented." Seeing his wife's obvious distress, John Rolfe suggested that the two men allow her time to recover her composure. At least two or three hours passed before Pocahontas had calmed down enough to properly greet her visitor.

Once the earlier emotional storm she had experienced at the first sight of Smith had calmed, Pocahontas was composed but clearly angry. One can only imagine all the emotions that had built up inside throughout the past eight years. Her questions may have come in bursts of words: Why had John Smith not visited her in London? Surely he had heard she was there. Had her father not helped Smith when he was new to Virginia? Why had he broken their agreements? "You did promise Powhatan what was yours should [be] his, and he the like to you," said Pocahontas. "You called him father being in his land a stranger."

Now a woman, confident and self-assured, Pocahontas was no longer the curious child that Smith had first encountered. Smith himself had aged; his hair was now tinged with gray, his face heavily lined. Caught up in a swirl of emotion, Pocahontas continued: Why had Smith

In fact, his appearance was so startling to Pocahontas that she was simply unable to speak.

let Pocahontas think he was dead all these many years? "They did tell us always you were dead, and I knew no other till I came to Plymouth," she reproached him. What of their adopted familial bond? Did it matter so little to Smith? Pocahontas reminded him of their kinship. There was little Smith could offer to dispel the fury unleashed by the woman standing before him. Instead he may have asked the obvious—inquiring about her father, the Virginia countryside he loved, what she had thought of England.

Smith's writings are the only first-person account of the meeting between these two individuals, and he simply recorded fragments of their conversation. Clearly, their time together had some awkward and difficult moments. But the fact that Smith detailed Pocahontas's anger and hurt about his behavior is somewhat astonishing. Although his records of the Jamestown years have been invaluable to historians, Smith did have a tendency to portray himself in a pretty positive light in his writings. In this instance, though, he was at fault and obviously felt badly about it. The visit between the two friends ended somewhat awkwardly. Much was left unsaid—perhaps because there simply were not enough words or maybe because there was not enough time. Regardless, when John Smith left, Pocahontas knew she would not see him again. Whatever had been left unsaid between them would remain that way for eternity.

No longer a young Indian maiden, the woman known as Rebecca Rolfe greeted John Smith as an equal. Some details of their emotionally charged final meeting appear in his later writings.

Even though she had grown very fond of the English countryside and wished to remain there, John Rolfe's business interests lay on the other side of the Atlantic, and they had to return.

Final Days of the Princess

Despite the worsening health of his wife and son—for Thomas was ill now, too—John Rolfe made the decision to set sail for Virginia in March. The Rolfes' stay in England had lasted long enough, and John Rolfe still felt optimistic that Pocahontas's health would improve once they were on their way back across the Atlantic. After first returning to London, those who had made the journey the year before boarded another of Samuel Argall's ships, the *George*. Too sick to remain on deck, Pocahontas and her son were taken to the Rolfes' sleeping quarters as the ship sailed away from the dock. But just twenty-five miles down the Thames—before the *George* had even reached the open waters of the Atlantic—it became apparent that Pocahontas could travel no farther. Although no specific details remain, some believe she may have suffered a tubercular hemorrhage (bleeding in the lungs).

At John Rolfe's request, Samuel Argall dropped anchor off the town of Gravesend, and Pocahontas was taken ashore to a local inn. Although a doctor was called, nothing could be done. True to her nature, Pocahontas thought of those other than herself. "All must die," she told her husband. "'Tis enough that the child liveth." With these final words, the life of Pocahontas ended. It was March 21, 1617; she was twenty-one.

True to her nature, Pocahontas thought of those other than herself.

A Christian funeral was held later the same day, and Pocahontas was laid to rest as Rebecca Rolfe. It is believed that she was buried in the **chancel** of St. George's church in Gravesend, but the structure was destroyed by fire in 1727. After the church was rebuilt, the exact location of Pocahontas's burial site was unknown. Today, a bronze statue of the Indian princess, with arms outstretched, is located in the churchyard; a duplicate of the same statue stands in Jamestown.

Now twice-widowed, a grief-stricken John Rolfe returned to the *George* and the ship continued farther downriver. Once again, Samuel Argall was asked to drop anchor when Rolfe realized his son was also too sick to make the lengthy Atlantic crossing.

Buried far from her Virginia homeland, Pocahontas is memorialized by this statue in the Gravesend churchyard. A twin statue stands at the Jamestown settlement.

Fearing he would lose Thomas as well, John Rolfe made the difficult decision to leave the two-year-old behind in England with his brother Henry. Although Thomas survived the illness, he remained with his uncle's family in England for his entire childhood. As an adult, Thomas Rolfe later traveled to America and settled, but he never saw his father again.

John Rolfe, to whom it seemed business may have been more important than family, returned safely to Virginia. His success as a tobacco planter continued to grow, and he became more involved in Virginia politics. He also remarried and had at least one other child. In 1622, Rolfe's plantation was destroyed in an Indian attack, and he died the same year.

Thomas Rolfe did not travel to the land of his mother's birth until 1635. Like the father he never knew, Thomas eventually became a very successful Virginia planter with thousands of acres of land—much of it left to him by his Native American grandfather, Powhatan. His descendents, who are also those of the Powhatan princess Pocahontas, are counted among Virginia's most distinguished families.

The Powhatan after Pocahontas

Chief Powhatan died in April 1618—only a year after his beloved daughter. Following his death, the period known as the Peace of Pocahontas came to an end. Opechancanough, the great chief's brother who had captured John Smith in 1607, took over as leader and waged a major attack on colonial settlements in 1622. For the next two decades, a series of skirmishes took place between the two sides. In 1644, Opechancanough made one final attempt to wipe out the English. Although hundreds of settlers died, Opechancanough's capture and death effectively ended the conflict.

The resulting treaties severely restricted the Powhatan people's movements, and their numbers dwindled to less than two thousand by the early eighteenth century. Many of those not killed in battle—or felled by diseases brought to Virginia by the English—fled north into areas of present-day New Jersey and Pennsylvania. However, some descendants of Chief Powhatan's great empire do still reside in Virginia. Today they are recognized as members of the Pamunkey, Mattaponi, and Chickahominy tribes.

After the deaths of Pocahontas and Powhatan, the period of peace among Indians and Europeans ended. This c. 1634 engraving depicts the 1622 massacre at Jamestown, during which more than 300 settlers lost their lives.

Legacy

What of the legacy of Pocahontas herself? Pocahontas is usually glorified in films and paintings as a dark-haired beauty often teamed with a handsome and dashing John Smith. After viewing these highly stylized images, many have automatically assumed a romance took place—despite the fact that nothing in history supports this assumption.

Sometimes history's attempts to glamorize the story of Pocahontas have overshadowed the actual details. Certainly her endeavors to assist the newly arrived English during the early

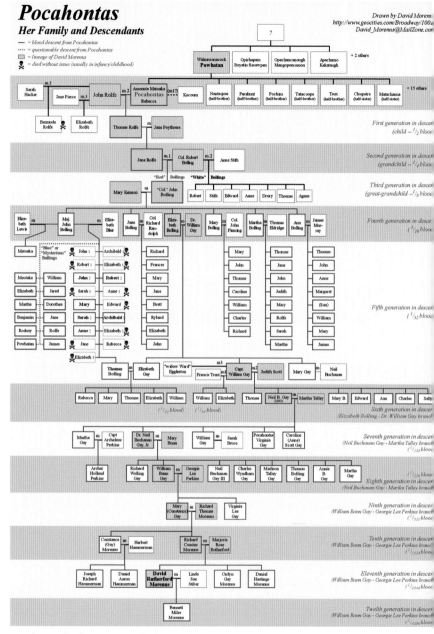

Pocahontas
Her Family and Descendants

Drawn by David Morenus
http://www.geocities.com/Broadway/100...
David_Morenus@MailZone.com

— = blood descent from Pocahontas
···· = questionable descent from Pocahontas
▢ = lineage of David Morenus
☇ = died without issue (usually in infancy/childhood)

Thousands of Americans today believe their roots go back to Pocahontas and her English husband, John Rolfe. One such proclaimed descendant is David Morenus, who put together this chart of Pocahontas's family and descendants.

Little in this stylized head-and-shoulders portrait of Pocahontas, portrayed here as Rebecca Rolfe, identifies the Powhatan princess's Native American heritage.

days of the Jamestown settlement are highly commendable. And it is considered even more remarkable because Pocahontas is usually thought of as operating completely alone and against the wishes of her people.

In truth, however, some credit must also be given to Chief Powhatan and his followers for their overall tolerance and periodic support of the colonists. Without it, Jamestown might have become another Lost Colony.

Regardless, nearly four centuries after her death, Pocahontas remains a fascinating figure. To have accomplished so much, taken so many risks, and considered others above herself so often, there is no doubt that she was an uncommon individual—especially in light of her youth. Pocahontas's story will certainly continue to serve as an inspiration for her people and those whose ancestors came to the New World from distant shores.

Glossary

aristocracy—a group or governing body usually made up of a small privileged class.

benefactor—a person who gives a gift or some form of help to people or institutions.

chancel—the space around an altar, usually enclosed by a railing or fence.

charter—a document, such as one from royalty, granting certain rights to a person or company.

contaminated—made impure or unclean.

coronation—the ceremony during which a new king, queen, or supreme ruler is installed.

entourage—a group that follows or attends to an important person.

flagship—the ship that carries the commander of a fleet.

hostage—a prisoner that is held to ensure that another person or organization meets specific terms.

mercenary—a person hired to fight for a country other than his or her own.

millstone—a circular stone used for grinding grain.

parsonage—the official residence provided by a church for its minister.

peninsula—a piece of land surrounded on three sides by water.

privateer—the captain of a privately owned warship.

ransom—payment demanded for the release of someone held captive.

rations—fixed portions of an item, usually of food, distributed during periods when supplies are short or demand is high.

symbolism—the use of an image to represent an idea, object, or event.

trade winds—persistent tropical winds found near the equator.

tribute—something done or given as an expression of respect or admiration.

vermin—small animals or insects; pests.

Bibliography

Books

Allen, Paula Gunn. *Pocahontas: Medicine Woman, Spy, Entrepreneur, Diplomat.* New York: HarperCollins, 2004.

Bruchac, Joseph. *Pocahontas.* San Diego: Houghton Mifflin Harcourt, 2003.

Campbell, Charles. *History of the Colony and Ancient Dominion of Virginia.* Philadelphia: J.B. Lippincott and Co., 1860.

Chenoweth, Avery and Robert Llewellyn. *Empires of the Forest: Jamestown and the Beginning of America.* Charlottesville: The University of Virginia Press, 2006.

Fritz, Jean. *The Double Life of Pocahontas.* New York: G. P. Putnam's Sons, 1983.

Iannone, Catherine. *Pocahontas: The True Story of the Powhatan Princess.* New York: Chelsea House, 1996.

Kelso, William M. *Jamestown: The Buried Truth*. Charlottesville: University of Virginia Press, 2006.

Kupperman, Karen Ordahl. *The Jamestown Project*. Cambridge: Harvard University Press, 2007.

Lankford, John, ed. *Captain John Smith's America: Selections from His Writings*. New York: Harper & Row, 1967.

Mossiker, Frances. *Pocahontas: The Life and the Legend*. New York: Alfred A. Knopf, 1976.

Price, David A. *Love and Hate in Jamestown: John Smith, Pocahontas, and the Heart of a New Nation*. New York: Alfred A. Knopf, 2003.

Smith, John. *Travels and Works of John Smith V1: President Of Virginia, And Admiral Of New England 1580–1631*. Edited by Edward Arber. Whitefish, MT: Kessinger Publishing, LLC, 2007.

———. *Writings: With Other Narratives of Roanoke, Jamestown, and the First English Settlement of America*. Edited by James P. P. Horn. New York: The Library of America, 2007.

Southern, Ed. *The Jamestown Adventure: Accounts of the Virginia Colony, 1605–1614*. Winston-Salem, NC: John F. Blair, Publisher, 2004.

Warner, Charles Dudley. *Captain John Smith (1579–1631) Sometimes Governor of Virginia, and Admiral of New England: A Study of His Life and Writings*. New York: H. Holt, 1881.

Woolley, Benjamin. *Savage Kingdom: The True Story of Jamestown, 1607, and the Settlement of America*. New York: HarperCollins, 2007.

Web sites

"Charter to Sir Walter Raleigh: 1584." The Avalon Project, Yale Law School, 2008. http://avalon.law.yale.edu/16th_century/raleigh.asp.

Cotton, Lee. "Powhatan Indian Lifeways," National Park Service, 1999. http://www.nps.gov/jame/historyculture/powhatan-indian-lifeways.htm.

Gallivan, Martin. "A Study of Virginia Indians and Jamestown: The First Century," National Park Service, November 2006. http://www.nps.gov/history/history/online_books/jame1/moretti-langholtz/chap3.htm.

Hatch, Charles E. Jr., Edward M. Riley. "James Towne: In the Words of Contemporaries," National Park Service, 1941. http://www.nps.gov/history/history/online_books/source/sb5/sb5b.htm.

"James River Plantations," National Park Service, http://www.nps.gov/history/nr/travel/jamesriver/colonization.htm.

"John Rolfe," Jamestown Rediscovery, The Association for the Preservation of Virginia Antiquities, 1995. http://www.apva.org/history/jrolfe.html.

Mann, Charles. "America, Found and Lost," *National Geographic*, May 2007. http://ngm.nationalgeographic.com/2007/05/jamestown/charles-mann-text.

"Pocahontas," Jamestown Rediscovery, The Association for the Preservation of Virginia Antiquities. http://www.apva.org/history/pocahont.html.

"Pocahontas Revealed," Documentary transcript, PBS, May 2007. http://www.pbs.org/wgbh/nova/transcripts/3407_pocahont.html.

Smith, John. Letter to Queen Anne of Great Britain in 1616, Digital History, 2009. http://www.digitalhistory.uh.edu/learning_history/pocahontas/pocahontas_smith_letter.cfm.

"Virtual Jamestown," http://www.virtualjamestown.org.

"What Did the Colonists Eat?" Jamestown Rediscovery, The Association for the Preservation of Virginia Antiquities, 2000. http://www.apva.org/exhibit/eats.html.

Source Notes

The following list identifies the sources of the quoted material found in this book. The first and last few words of each quotation are cited, followed by the source. Complete information on each source can be found in the Bibliography.

Abbreviations:

AMER—"America, Found and Lost"

BUR—*Jamestown: The Buried Truth*

CJS—*Captain John Smith (1579–1631) Sometimes Governor of Virginia, and Admiral of New England: A Study of His Life and Writings*

CJSA—*Captain John Smith's America: Selections from His Writings*

CJSW—*Captain John Smith Writings*

CON—"James Towne: In the Words of Contemporaries"

DBL—*The Double Life of Pocahontas*

EMP—*Empires of the Forest*

HCV—*History of the Colony and Ancient Dominion of Virginia*

JA—*The Jamestown Adventure: Accounts of the Virginia Colony, 1605–1614*

JAM—"James River Plantations"

JP—*The Jamestown Project*

LOVE—*Love and Hate in Jamestown*

PB—*Pocahontas*

PIL—"Powhatan Indian Lifeways"

PJR—"Pocahontas," Jamestown Rediscovery

POC—*Pocahontas: The Life and the Legend*

PWC—*Pocahontas: Medicine Woman, Spy, Entrepreneur, Diplomat*

QUEEN—John Smith's Letter to Queen Anne of Great Britain in 1616

REV—"Pocahontas Revealed"

ROLFE—"John Rolfe"

SAV—*Savage Kingdom*

STUDY—"A Study of Virginia Indians and Jamestown: The First Century"

SWR—"Charter to Sir Walter Raleigh: 1584"

TRUE—*Pocahontas: The True Story of the Powhatan Princess*

TW—*Travels and Works of John Smith V1: President Of Virginia, And Admiral Of New England 1580–1631*

VIR—"Virtual Jamestown"

INTRODUCTION: Different Worlds

    PAGE 1 *"During the time of . . . utter confusion.":* JP, p. 234

CHAPTER 1: The Powhatan People

    PAGE 2 *"History is the memory of . . . the living.":* TW

    PAGE 3 *"remote, heathen, and barbarous lands . . . Christian people":* SWR

    PAGE 4 *"a tall, well-proportioned man . . . hardy body":* PIL

    PAGE 4 *"well beaten . . . clean limbs":* AMER

    PAGES 4–5 *"It is strange . . . he commands":* STUDY

CHAPTER 2: The Child Matoaka
PAGE 12 *"A child of . . . [Powhatan's] people"*: VIR
PAGE 13 *"people clothed with . . . their middles."*: JAM

CHAPTER 3: From Across the Sea
PAGE 21 *". . . the winds continued . . . or danger"*: JA, p. 23
PAGE 24 *"gentlemen,"*: LOVE, p. 4
PAGE 28 *"there came the savages . . . very desperately"*: SAV, p. 56
PAGE 31 *"a very fit place . . . a great [city]."*: BUR, p. 14

CHAPTER 4: Jamestown
PAGE 32 *"Heaven and earth . . . man's habitation."*: POC, p. 10
PAGE 33 *"Now [falls] every man. . . . some nets."*: BUR, p. 15
PAGE 36 *"came up almost into . . . the tents."*: PB, p. 52
PAGE 38 *"within less than seven. . . . our proceedings."*: JA, p. 19
PAGE 38 *"they would rather starve . . . without constraint."*: PB, p. 106

CHAPTER 5: Smith's Capture
PAGE 42 *"At last they . . . their Emperor."*: POC, p. 77
PAGE 42 *"love[d] children very dearly."*: CJSA, p. 20
PAGE 49 *"Before a fire . . . hanging by,"*: EMP, p. 69
PAGE 51 *"generally beautiful . . . shape and features."*: PIL
PAGE 52 *"a long consultation . . . [his] brains"*: CJSW, p. 321

CHAPTER 6: A Fateful Meeting
PAGE 53 *"Had the Savages . . . [would have] starved"*: VIR
PAGE 60 *"Everything my son . . . off the ship"*: LOVE, p. 72
PAGE 61 *"bread . . . wild beasts"*: POC, p. 91

CHAPTER 7: Strained Relations
PAGE 63 *". . . I also am . . . my land."*: POC, p. 115
PAGE 68 *"abundance of fish . . . frying pan."*: POC, p. 106

CHAPTER 8: Troubled Times
PAGE 72 *"He that will . . . not [eat]."*: POC, p. 108
PAGE 72 *"thirty Carpenters . . . of trees."*: POC, p. 117
PAGE 73 *". . . my country . . . to go from you."*: HCV, p. 114
PAGE 80 *"tore the flesh. . . . nearly drowned."*: CJS, p.179

CHAPTER 9: On Her Own
PAGE 82 *"Pocahontas lay concealed . . . but trusty Friends."*: POC, p. 151

CHAPTER 10: A Changed Life
PAGE 91 *". . . for the good of . . . mine own salvation. . . ."*: VIR
PAGE 91 *"that I had taken . . . otherwise not."*: LOVE, p. 150
PAGE 91 *"despondent and pensive"*: EMP, p. 154
PAGE 92 *"very well and [kindly treated]."*: POC, p. 161
PAGE 95 *"expressed an . . . in learning."*: POC, p. 167
PAGE 96 *"It is Pocahontas . . . intricate a labyrinth."*: POC, p. 161
PAGE 97 *"pleasant, [sweet], and strong,"*: ROLFE

CHAPTER 11: Rebecca Rolfe
PAGE 100 *"At last rejecting . . . English Gentleman."*: QUEEN
PAGE 101 *"She lives civilly . . . with him."*: POC, p. 193
PAGE 103 *"as the stars . . . leaves on the trees."*: POC, p. 68

CHAPTER 12: Death on English Soil

PAGE 109 *"... I will be ... your countryman."*: PWC, p. 292

PAGE 109 *"Without any words ... well contented."*: REV

PAGE 109 *"You did promise. ... land a stranger."*: TRUE, p. 71

PAGE 110 *"They did tell us ... to Plymouth."*: TRUE, p. 71

PAGE 112 *"All must die. ... the child liveth."*: PJR

Image Credits

About the Author

Victoria Garrett Jones is a freelance writer and former National Geographic Society researcher. The author of three Sterling Biographies, on Eleanor Roosevelt, Marian Anderson, and Amelia Earhart, Jones lives with her husband and two children on Maryland's Eastern Shore. This is her eighth publication for Sterling Publishing.

Index